招き猫
maneki-neko
lucky cat

寿司
sushi
sushi

冷やし中華
hiyashi chūka
cold ramen noodles

抹茶
matcha
green tea powder

餃子
gyōza
dumplings

盆栽
bonsai
a miniature tree
in tray

ラーメン
rāmen
egg noodles
in pork broth

下駄
geta
wooden clogs

JAPANESE
PICTURE
DICTIONARY

LEARN 1,500 JAPANESE WORDS AND PHRASES

Timothy G Stout

TUTTLE Publishing

Tokyo | Rutland, Vermont | Singapore

Contents

A Basic Introduction to
the Japanese Language   4

1 Nice to Meet You!   10
はじめまして！

2 My Family   12
私の家族

3 My House   14
私の家

4 The Human Body   16
人間の体

5 Counting and Numbers   18
数を数える

6 Daily Activities   20
日常生活

7 Colors and Shapes   22
色と形

8 Opposites   24
反対語

9 Talking about Money   26
お金について話す

10 Going Shopping   28
買い物へ行く

11 Life in the City   30
街の生活

12 Around Town   32
街で

13 Asking Directions 34
道を尋ねる

14 Telling about the Weather 36
天気について話す

15 Telling Time 38
時間について話す

16 Years and Dates 40
年と日付

17 Four Seasons 42
四季

18 Celebrating the Holidays 44
祝日を祝う

19 I Love to Learn 46
学ぶのが好き

20 At School 48
学校で

21 Learning Japanese 50
日本語を学ぶ

22 Counting Words 52
助数詞

23 Computers and the Internet 54
コンピューターと
インターネット

24 My Smartphone 56
私のスマホ

25 At Work 58
職場で

26 Music and Dance 60
音楽と踊り

How to Download the Online Audio
recordings for this Book.

1. Make sure you have an Internet connection.
2. Type the URL below into your web browser.

http://www.tuttlepublishing.com/japanese-picture-
dictionary-downloadable-content

For support, you can email us at info@tuttlepublishing.com.

27 Seeing a Doctor 62
医者に診てもらう

28 Protecting Our Environment 64
環境を守る

29 The Animal Kingdom 66
動物界

30 Let's Keep Fit! 68
健康を保とう！

31 Do You Like to Travel? 70
旅行が好き？

32 Countries of the World 72
世界の国々

33 Foreign Languages 74
外国語

34 Do You Like Japanese Food? 76
和食は好き？

35 Popular Western Foods 78
人気の洋食

36 Drinks 80
飲み物

37 Fresh Fruits, Nuts and Grains 82
果物、ナッツ、穀類

38 At the Market 84
スーパーで

English-Japanese Index 87

A Basic Introduction to the Japanese Language

This picture dictionary introduces approximately 1,650 high-frequency Japanese words and phrases, and it was made with you, the learner, in mind. Whether you are studying the language in a traditional classroom setting, or simply interested in the beauty of the Japanese language, this book has something for you.

Visual learners will appreciate the graphic layout, and aural learners will enjoy using the audio files that include all 1,650 words and phrases in Japanese and English, read by a native speaker of each, respectively. Verbal learners will be drawn to the topic-based and list-oriented organization. This book may be optimally used by both English speaking learners of Japanese, as well as by Japanese speaking learners of English.

This picture dictionary is comprised of high-frequency words ideal for those taking the Japanese Language Proficiency Test (JLPT) levels 4 and 5 administered by the Japanese government. It is also designed for students taking the AP Japanese Language and Culture exam administered by the College Board and Educational Testing Services in the United States.

Level 5 of the JLPT requires knowledge of approximately 700 words and Level 4 of the JLPT requires knowledge of an additional 900 words. In order to obtain command of the approximately 1,600 words needed to pass the JLPT Level 4, learners must focus on vocabulary. Combined with any regular first year college textbook, this book will greatly assist students who wish to pass the JLPT.

The AP Japanese Language and Culture exam assesses the proficiency of students, assuming the equivalent of two years study at the college level. The AP Japanese exam is geared between the JLPT Level 4 and Level 3. This book covers all of the most important vocabulary, in combination with the regular AP Japanese studies.

Japanese is spoken by 130 million people in Japan, and hundreds of thousands of others living throughout the world. The Japanese have a unique 2000-year-old culture, enjoyed by many millions of people who have developed an appreciation for anime, manga, Japanese music, movies, and literature. This book will help you better understand this unique and wonderful language and culture, opening doors that cannot be opened in any other way.

Basics of the Japanese language

The Japanese sounds system is not difficult for speakers of English to learn. There are five basic vowel sounds:

> A (あ) as in "at"
> I (い) as in "ink"
> U (う) as in "blue"
> E (え) as in "egg"
> O (お) as in "oats"

In addition to the five vowel sounds, there are 13 basic consonant sounds, plus three special consonant sounds, which will be introduced below.

> K   as in "kit" combines with the five vowels: KA, KI, KU, KE, KO (かきくけこ).
> S   as in "sit" combines with the fives vowels: SA, SHI, SU, SE, SO (さしすせそ).
>   Note that S changes to SH as in "she" when paired with the vowel I. There is no SI sound in Japanese.
> T   as in "tip" combines with the five vowels: TA, CHI, TSU, TE, and TO (たちつてと).
>   Note that T changes to CH as in "cheerful" when paired with the vowel I. There is no TI sound in Japanese. Also, note that T changes to TS as in "tsunami" when paired with the vowel U. There is no TU sound in Japanese.
> N   as in "nap" combines with the five vowels: NA, NI, NU, NE, NO (なにぬねの).
> H   as in "hat" combines with the five vowels: HA, HI, FU, HE, HO (はひふへほ).

Note that H changes to F when combined with the vowel U. It actually sounds a bit like the English word "who" but with lips more rounded, and more breath.

M as in "mat" combines with the five vowels: MA, MI, MU, ME, MO (まみむめも).

Y as in "yes" combines with only three vowels: YA, YU, YO (やゆよ).

There is no YI or YE sound in modern Japanese.

R is tricky to say for English speakers, and can be describe as blend of the English "L" and "D". Perhaps luckily, there is no L sound in Japanese. To make this sounds let your tongue touch the roof of your mouth, and then move forward as the sound is made, similar to when you are pronouncing an L or D.

R is paired with the five vowels: RA, RI, RU, RE, RO (らりるれろ).

G as in "get" combines with the five vowels: GA, GI, GU, GE, GO (がぎぐげご).

Z as in "zoo" combines with the five vowels: ZA, JI, ZU, ZE, ZO (ざじずぜぞ).

Note that Z changes to J when paired with I. There is no ZI sound in Japanese.

D as in "dot" combines with the five vowels: DA, JI, ZU, DE, DO (だぢづでど).

Note that D also changes to J when paired with I. There is no DI sound in Japanese. In addition, note that D also changes to Z when paired with U. There is no DU sound in Japanese. That's right, there are two ways to write JI and ZU. You can know which one to use, depending on the word.

B as in "bat" combines with the five vowels: BA, BI, BU, BE, BO (ばびぶべぼ).

P as in "pan" combines with the five vowels: PA, PI, PU, PE, PO (ぱぴぷぺぽ).

In addition to the 5 basic vowels and 16 basic consonant sounds in Japanese, there are 33 "blended" sounds that result when you combine YA, YU, YO (やゆよ) with 11 consonants.

KYA, KYU, KYO (きゃ、きゅ、きょ)	GYA, GYU, GYO (ぎゃ、ぎゅ、ぎょ)
SHA, SHU, SHO (しゃ、しゅ、しょ)	JA, JU, JO (じゃ、じゅ、じょ)
CHA, CHU, CHO (ちゃ、ちゅ、ちょ)	
NYA, NYU, NYO (にゃ、にゅ、にょ)	
HYA, HYU, HYO (ひゃ、ひゅ、ひょ)	BYA, BYU, BYO (びゃ、びゅ、びょ)
MYA, MYU, MYO (みゃ、みゅ、みょ)	PYA, PYU, PYO (ぴゃ、ぴゅ、ぴょ)
RYA, RYU, RYO (りゃ、りゅ、りょ)	

There are a few additional "spelling" rules to be aware of. These include the small tsu っ, long vowels, and three hiragana that make a sound change, when used as particles (wa は, e へ, o を). These rules will be explained below.

A small "TSU" (っ) is pronounced as a short silent pause. In rōmaji it is usually indicated by a doubling of the following consonant. One exception is the consonant "CH," in which case it is indicated by adding a "T" as in "DOTCHI" どっち or "which one; which way." A small "TSU" may also be used at the end of a phrase or sentence to indicate a sense of abruptness, anger, or surprise. In this case it is pronounced with a "glottal stop" or in other words, stopping the flow of air by closing the back of the throat (epiglottis).

As you may have noticed, some words in rōmaji have a line above a vowel, indicating it is a long vowel, or a vowel two syllables in length. Writing most long vowels in hiragana is simple; you add one of the five Japanese vowels あ, い, う, え, or お. As already noted, in rōmaji it is indicated by a line above the vowel, except, "I" which is written twice. Read the examples below.

Long "A"	おかあさん	O KĀ SA N	(mother)
Long "I"	いいえ	I I E	(no)
Long "U"	きゅうり	KYŪ RI	(cucumber)
Long "E"*	おねえさん	O NĒ SA N	(older sister)
Long "O"*	おおきい	Ō KI I	(big)

*Actually, the last two examples are exceptions. Usually い ("I" as in Hawaii) makes the long え ("E" as in red) sound. Take extra care to pronounce an い following a character with the え vowel sound as a long vowel え. At first, this may be a bit confusing because in rōmaji it is usually written with an "I." In this case the rōmaji convention reflects the hiragana writing, not the pronunciation.

えいご	E I GO	(English)
せんせい	SE N SE I	(teacher)
えいが	E I GA	(movie)
とけい	TO KE I	(clock)

Likewise, a long vowel お ("O" as in oak) is made by adding う ("U" as in glue). This book consistently uses a line above the "O" to indicate the long vowel in rōmaji "ō."

さようなら	SA YŌ NA RA	(goodbye)
ありがとう	A RI GA TŌ	(thank you)
もう いちど	MŌ I CHI DO	(one more time)

Japanese uses small grammatical words called "particles" to help the reader understand the relationships between words in a sentence. They are usually one or two hiragana characters in length, and they indicate the topic, subject, object, location, direction, and many other functions. Particles are always placed directly after the words they mark. This last rule simply describes how three hiragana characters are pronounced differently when used as sentence particles.

"WA (は)" The Topic Particle: When used as a "topic" particle, は is pronounced "WA (は)" instead of "HA." For example,

> I am a student.
> **Watashi wa gakusei desu.**
> 私は学生です。

"E (へ)" The Direction Particle: When used as a "direction" particle, へ is pronounced like え ("E" as in red) instead of "HE." For example,

> We are going to Peace Park (Hiroshima).
> **Watashitachi wa heiwa kōen e ikimasu.**
> 私たちは平和公園へ行きます。

"O (を)" The Object Particle: The character を is only used as a particle to mark the "object" of a sentence, and although it is in the "W" row of hiragana, it is pronounced as お ("O" as in oak). For example,

> I saw Mount Fuji.
> **Watashi wa fujisan o mimashita.**
> 私は富士山を見ました。

Japanese vocabulary

Vocabulary items, correctly pronounced, are the basic building blocks of fluency in any foreign language, and this is true of Japanese, as well. This book introduces 1,650 high-frequency words and expressions, that can help readers in many ways as they strive to develop their proficiency. It can be an excellent supplement to any Japanese textbook, which typically do not contain nearly as many vocabulary items, but rather focus more on grammar.

Japanese words come from three main sources: original Japanese words (**wago**), Chinese-Japanese words (**kango**), and foreign loan words (**gairaigo**). Original Japanese words are the basis of Japanese vocabulary and grammar, and they often have three or more syllables, such as the numbers 1, 2, 3 pronounced, **hitotsu**, **futatsu**, **mittsu** (ひとつ、ふたつ、みっつ). Chinese-Japanese words make up large portion of the language, and usually have one or two syllables, such as the numbers 1, 2, 3 pronounced, **ichi**, **ni**, **san** (いち、に、さん). The first set of numbers are used as general counters, whereas the second set are used for the abstract numbers and math, as well as other specific counters, such as age, time, and money. Foreign loan words include the majority of new words that have entered the Japanese language in the past 200 years, including words relating to modern life, science, and technology. Examples include, shower, **shawā** (シャワー), recycling, **risaikuru** (リサイクル), and TV, **terebi** (テレビ).

No matter where Japanese words originated from, they all conform to the simple sounds of the Japanese language. This is why foreigners often do not recognize Chinese-Japanese words or foreign loan words, even if they speak Chinese or the foreign language from which these word originated. Still, since the Japanese sound system is simple, learning to pronounce these words is simple. Keep working at it, and you will be pronouncing Japanese words correctly in no time!

Japanese grammar

Japanese grammar is quite different from English. The general word order is, subject-object-verb or SOV, whereas English is, subject-verb-object or SVO. For example, in English we say, John kicked the ball, but in Japanese we say, John the ball kicked. If you are familiar with Yoda the little green character in George Lucus' Star Wars films, and will recall that he often speaks with a distinctive word order similar to Japanese, such as, "Patience, you must have." Perhaps Lucas patterned Yoda's speech patterns after the Japanese language.

Japanese has several dozen common particles—one or two syllable words that clarify parts of speech. There are particles that indicate which word is the topic (**wa** は), subject (**ga** が), and object (**o** を). There are particles that indicate specific time (**ni** に), a location of action (**de** で), and direction (**e** へ). Perhaps because particles make parts of speech very clear, Japanese grammar is also more flexble when it comes to word order. As long as the verb or predicate comes last in the sentence, the other words are generally free to be aranged in any way that meets the individual speaker's needs.

Japanese is also a topic-prominent language, meaning that speakers are usually aware of the topic of any given sentence, and this influences the way they express themselves. For example, once a topic is mentioned, and enters into the discourse, the speakers may freely omit it from their speech, until the topic is changed or it becomes less clear, and must be restated. Omitting the topic from the sentence in Japanese can be confusing to learners at first, but it also helps the language be much more efficient.

The Japanese writing system

Japanese uses four types of scripts: hiragana, katakana, kanji, and rōmaji (as noted, the line above the "o" indicates it is two syllables in length). Hiragana is a cursive set of 46 phonetic characters that express all of the sounds of Japanese. It is mainly used for writing the grammatical parts of sentences and native Japanese words that there are no kanji for. Katakana is an angular set of 46 phonetic characters, generally used for foreign words and for showing emphasis. Kanji are characters of ancient Chinese origin that represent ideas and sounds, and they are used for most nouns, verbs, and other "content" words. There are 2,136 "common use" kanji that school children must learn by ninth grade. Rōmaji are roman (Latin) letters used to write Japanese; you must already know rōmaji since you are reading this. Rōmaji is used in textbooks and dictionaries for foreigners learning Japanese (and for Japanese people learning western languages) but their use in day-to-day writing is somewhat limited to things such as company names and acronyms.

ひらがな **Hiragana**	カタカナ **Katakana**	漢字 **Kanji**	Rōmaji **Romanized Japanese**

Japanese hiragana and katakana

There are various styles used to write hiragana, but this book only uses the most standard kyōkasho-tai or "schoolbook" style. Every hiragana character is composed of up to three types of strokes called "stops," "jumps," and "brushes." With a stop the pencil must come to a stop, as the name implies, before it is removed from the paper. Jumps are written by removing the pencil from the paper as it moves to the next stroke. With a brush the pencil is slowly removed from the paper as the stroke is written, giving it a tapered, sweeping appearance. In the example below, the character "KE (け)" as in "ketchup" is written with all three types of strokes. The first stroke is a jump, the second is a stop, and the third is a brush.

Writing the correct stroke types in the correct order is important for forming balanced, legible characters. With practice you will get the hang of it. You can make your characters look more authentic by slightly tilting left-to-right strokes, as in stroke two in "KE" (see above right), rather than writing them straight across. Character strokes are generally written from left to right and top to bottom. Try to center each character in the center of an imaginary box, not too far to the left, right, top, or bottom (see brloe).

け	け	け	け	け
Correct!	Wrong	Wrong	Wrong	Wrong

Traditionally Japanese was written from top to bottom, progressing in columns from right to left across the page. These days it is commonly written from left to right, as with English. All the Japanese in this book is written from left to right.

Japanese Kanji

Japanese kanji characters originally came from China, where hanzi characters were first used approximately 5000 years ago. The word "kanji" is a Japanese approximation of the Chinese word, "hanzi," which can be broken into two parts, "han," meaning the Han Chinese people, who make up 90 percent of the population of China, and "zi" which means character. Kanji literally means, "Han characters." Of course, today they are used in various forms by many millions of people around the world.

Japanese kanji can be divided into four basic types: 1) pictographs (pictures of objects), 2) ideographs (pictures of ideas, such as "up," "down," "inside," and "outside"), 3) pictograph compounds (for example, three "trees" represents "forest"), and 4) sound-ideograph compounds (combination of characters used for their sound and other characters used for their meaning). There are relatively few characters of the first three types. Approximately 90 percent of kanji are sound-ideograph compounds. Understanding this will help you learn Japanese characters more effectively.

1. Pictographs	2. Ideograms	3. Pictograph compounds	4. Sound–ideograph compounds
山、田、川	三、上、中	森、町、物	英、語、曜
Mountain, rice field, river	Three, up, inside	Forest, town, thing	English, language, day of the week

Kanji often appear alone, but they more often appear in strings of two or more kanji, called compounds. In this way the 2,136 "regular use" kanji are combined to make tens of thousands of Japanese words. Most of these compounds came this way from China. Some of them were invented in Japan. Occasionally, new kanji invented in Japan and then adopted in China. Although these common compounds share the same meanings, their pronunciations are different. Unlike Chinese, the Japanese kanji usually have many pronunciations for each kanji, depending on the context. The chart below shows how one kanji combines with various other kanji to create new words, many of which have different pronunciations.

Kanji	Meaning	Reading	Compounds	Second Kanji meanings	Compound Meanings	Compound Readings
今	Now	いま (**ima**)	今日 今週 今月 今年	日 (day) 週 (week) 月 (month) 年 (year)	Today This week This month This year	きょう (**kyō**) こんしゅう (**konshū**) こんげつ (**kongetsu**) ことし (**kotoshi**)

Focus on vocabulary

As visually interesting as the Japanese writing system is, beginning learners should not become overly concerned with it, and neglect the development of a strong vocabulary in Japanese. Beginning learners will need at least many hundred, and intermediate learners will need around two thousand. This book focuses on vocabulary, and will be a huge help to you with this goal.

How to use this book

This book contains 38 topics, filled with high-frequency words to help boost your Japanese proficiency at the beginning and intermediate levels. You can use it in a few ways, depending on your goals. One way is to use it in conjunction with a traditional textbook to greatly expand your vocabulary. Another way is to simply use it on its own as an enrichment tool for your personal studies. Either way, it is a useful resource, which taken with the included audio files (a link to download the audio files can be found on page 96), will help you master hundreds of useful vocabulary and phrases.

Many readers will find this a perfect supplement to their regular Japanese studies. Whether with a formal class, or studing on your own, having a comprehensive vocabulary resource is crucial to improving overall proficiency. You can begin with your grammar book or textbook, and then turn to a given topic in this book for additional useful words and phrases not contained in the regular textbook. Alternatively, you can start with this book, in order to boost your vocabulary knowledge, allowing yourself to express yourself more fully in the topics found in your regular grammar book or textbook.

Some readers will simply enjoy browsing through this picture dictionary. Whether as a beginner or as an intermediate learner, this book has something for you. Glancing through the book, you will quickly notice the breadth of the words and phrases associated with the many highly relevant topics it contains. For beginners it may be your first taste of the sound and structure of Japanese. For more advanced students, it may simply be a refresher of these topics, within which you are likely to find numerous items that you did not know, or perhaps had forgotten. Regardless, it is sure to enrich your learning, and help you take the next step in your pathway to proficiency.

The index at the end of the book will help you find the meanings of words you have learned, but which you may have forgotten. The following information is included for each entry—the English word, the Japanese word, the romanization, the lesson number and the order in which the word appeared in that lesson, followed by the page number where the word appears. For example:

English word	Japanese	Romanization	Lesson and order	Page in book
smartwatch	スマートウォッチ	**sumātowotchi**	[15-14]	39

はじめまして！

Hajimemashite!

Nice to Meet You!

1 こんにちは、
おげんきですか。
Konnichiwa. Ogenki desu ka.
Hello, how are you?

2 げんきです。ありがとう。
Genki desu. Arigatō.
I am fine, thank you!

3 会う
au
to meet

4 田中さん、こちらは山田さん です。
Tanaka-san, kochira wa Yamada-san desu.
Ms. Tanaka, this is Mr. Yamada.

5 はじめまして。
Hajimemashite.
Nice to meet you.

6 どうぞ、よろしく。
Dōzo yoroshiku.
Nice to meet you, too.

7 紹介する
shōkai suru
to introduce

8 何ですか?
Nan desu ka?
What?

9 満足
manzoku
satisfied

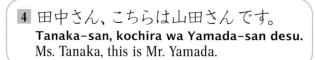

10 嬉しい
ureshii
happy

11 幸せ
shiawase
joyful

12 呼ぶ
yobu
to call;
to be called

13 祝う
iwau
to congratulate;
to celebrate

15 私の名前はスミスです。お名前は？
Watashi no namae wa sumisu desu. Onamae wa?
Hi, my name is Smith. What's your name?

16 私は川田ゆかです。名刺です。どうぞ。
Watashi wa Kawada Yuka desu. Meishi desu. Dōzo.
My name is Kawada Yuka. Here's my namecard.

14 自己紹介する
jikoshōkai suru
introduce yourself

17 じゃあね！さよなら！
Jā ne! Sayonara!
Goodbye! See you!

18 気をつけて！
Ki o tsukete!
Take care!

Additional Vocabulary

23 名前
namae
name

24 苗字
myōji
surname

25 貴方
anata
you (polite)

26 知る
shiru
to know

27 国籍
kokuseki
nationality

28 握手する
akushu suru
to shake hands

29 抱きあう
dakiau
to hug

30 キスする；
接吻する
**kisu suru;
seppun suru**
to kiss

31 笑う
warau
to smile

32 手を振る
te o furu
to wave

33 お辞儀を
する
ojigi o suru
to bow

34 挨拶をする
aisatsu o suru
to greet

35 話しかける
**hanashi-
kakeru**
to start a
conversation

36 おしゃべり
する
oshaberi suru
to make small
talk

37 話す
hanasu
to talk

38 どうですか?
Dō desu ka?
How are things?

39 どうして?；
なぜ?
**Dōshite?;
Naze?**
Why?

40 友達
tomodachi
friends

19 ミーティング
miitingu
gathering; meeting

20 お客さん
okyakusan
guest; customer

21 ありがとうございます！
Arigatō gozaimasu!
Thank you!

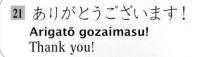

22 どういたしまして。
Dō itashimashite.
You're welcome.

11

2 私の家族
Watashi no kazoku
My Family

3 女性
josei
female

1 息子
musuko
son

2 男性
dansei
male

5 娘
musume
daughter

4 子ども
kodomo
children

6 両親
ryōshin
parents

Additional Vocabulary

26 妻
tsuma
wife

27 夫
otto
husband

28 娘婿；
義理の息子
**musume–muko;
giri no musuko**
son-in-law

29 嫁；義理の娘
**yome;
giri no musume**
daughter-in-law

30 孫；孫娘
**mago;
mago–musume**
grandson;
granddaughter

31 親戚
shinseki
relatives

32 隣人
rinjin
neighbor

33 義理の兄弟
giri no kyōdai
brother-in-law

34 義理の姉妹
giri no shimai
sister-in-law

35 家族
kazoku
family

36 自分
jibun
self

37 年下の
toshishita no
young

38 熱心な
nesshin na
enthusiastic

39 信じる
shinjiru
to believe

40 兄弟は何人いますか。
Kyōdai wa nan–nin imasu ka.
How many brothers and sisters do you have?

41 姉が一人と弟が一人います。
Ane ga hitori to otōto ga hitori imasu.
I have one elder sister and one younger brother.

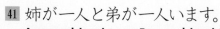

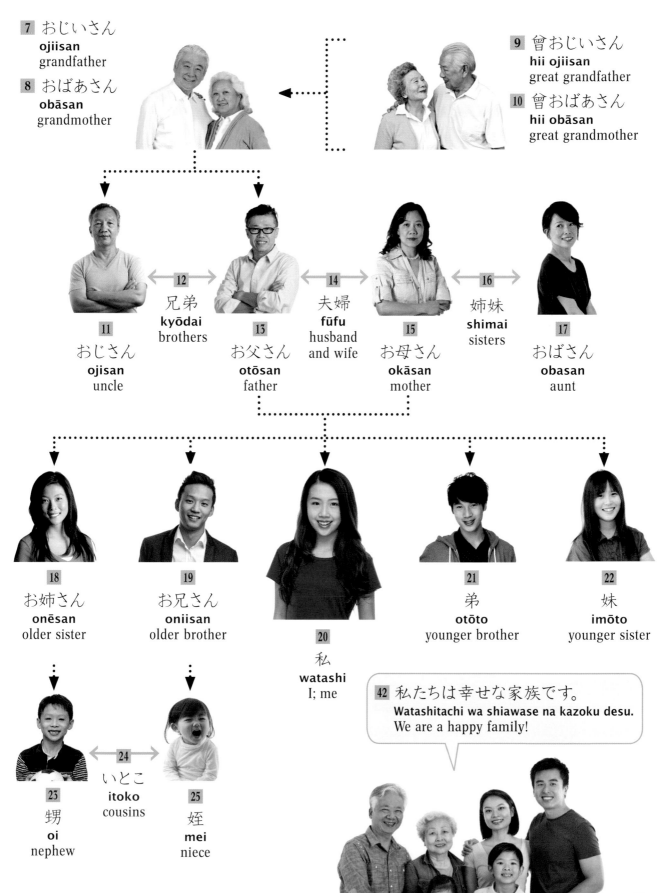

7 おじいさん
ojiisan
grandfather

8 おばあさん
obāsan
grandmother

9 曾おじいさん
hii ojiisan
great grandfather

10 曾おばあさん
hii obāsan
great grandmother

12 兄弟
kyōdai
brothers

14 夫婦
fūfu
husband
and wife

16 姉妹
shimai
sisters

11 おじさん
ojisan
uncle

13 お父さん
otōsan
father

15 お母さん
okāsan
mother

17 おばさん
obasan
aunt

18 お姉さん
onēsan
older sister

19 お兄さん
oniisan
older brother

20 私
watashi
I; me

21 弟
otōto
younger brother

22 妹
imōto
younger sister

23 甥
oi
nephew

24 いとこ
itoko
cousins

25 姪
mei
niece

42 私たちは幸せな家族です。
Watashitachi wa shiawase na kazoku desu.
We are a happy family!

13

私の家
Watashi no ie
3 My House

1 居間
ima
living room

2 バルコニー
barukonii
balcony

3 手すり
tesuri
railing

4 天井
tenjō
ceiling

5 鍵
kagi
keys

6 絵画
kaiga
painting

7 ランプ
Rampu
lamp

8 椅子
isu
chair

9 壁
kabe
wall

10 テレビ
terebi
television

11 コーヒー
テーブル
kōhi tēburu
coffee table

12 絨毯
jūtan
carpet

13 エアコン
eakon
air conditioner

14 テーブル
tēburu
table

15 ソファ
sofa
sofa

16 床
yuka
floor

17 カーテン
kāten
curtain

18 窓
mado
window

19 枕
makura
pillow

20 ベッド
beddo
bed

21 寝室
shinshitsu
bedroom

22 部屋
heya
room

Additional Vocabulary

49 電気の
スイッチ
denki no suitchi
light switch

50 コンセント
konsento
electric socket;
power point

51 家
ie; uchi
home; house

52 アパート
apāto
apartment

53 屋根
yane
roof

54 屋根裏
yaneura
attic; loft

55 地下
chika
basement; cellar

56 車庫
shako
garage

57 玄関
genkan
entrance

58 きれいな家ですね。住んでみたいです。
Kirei na ie desu ne. Sunde mitai desu.
What a beautiful house. I would love to
live here.

23 台所
daidokoro
kitchen

24 電子レンジ
denshi renji
microwave oven

28 レンジフード
renji hūdo
cooker hood

25 戸棚
todana
cabinet

29 やかん
yakan
kettle

26 冷蔵庫
reizōko
refrigerator

30 トースター
tōsutā
toaster

44 掃除する
sōji suru
to clean

27 オーブン
ōbun
oven

31 ストーブ
sutōbu
stove

32 勉強部屋
benkyō-beya
study room

33 電気スタンド
denki sutando
table lamp

34 引き出し
hikidashi
drawer

35 本棚
hondana
book shelf

45
エレベーター
erebētā
elevator

46
ドア
doa
door

36 机
tsukue
desk

47 鉢植え
hachiue
potted plant

37 浴室
yokushitsu
bathroom

38 お手洗い; トイレ
otearai; toire
washroom

41 シャワー
shawā
shower

48 入浴する
nyūyoku suru
to bathe

39 蛇口
jaguchi
water tap

42 お風呂; 浴槽
ofuro; yokusō
bathtub

40 洗面台
senmendai
sink

43 便器
benki
toilet bowl

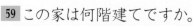

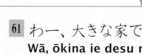

59 この家は何階建てですか。
Kono ie wa nangai-date desu ka.
How many floors does this house have?

61 わー、大きな家ですね！
Wā, ōkina ie desu ne!
What a big house!

60 私はアパートを借りたいです。
Watashi wa apāto o karitai desu.
I would like to rent an apartment.

62 台所を見せてください。
Daidokoro o misete kudasai.
Please show me the kitchen.

15

人間の体

Ningen no karada

The Human Body

4

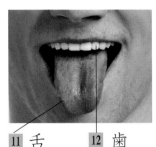

6 髪
kami
hair

7 眉毛
mayuge
eyebrow

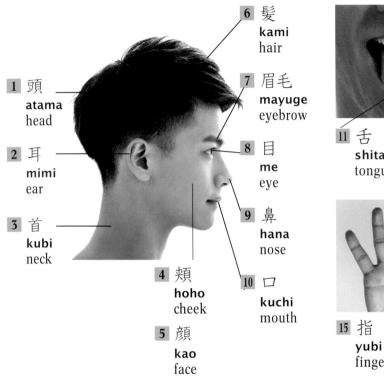

1 頭
atama
head

2 耳
mimi
ear

3 首
kubi
neck

8 目
me
eye

9 鼻
hana
nose

4 頬
hoho
cheek

10 口
kuchi
mouth

5 顔
kao
face

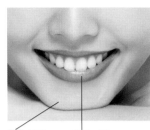

11 舌
shita
tongue

12 歯
ha
teeth

13 顎
ago
chin

14 唇
kuchibiru
lips

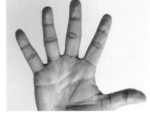

15 指
yubi
fingers

16 足指
ashiyubi
toes

---

50 体の部分をいくつ言えますか。
Karada no bubun o ikutsu iemasu ka.
How many parts of your body can you name?

51 どのように体を大事にして（扱って）いますか。
Dono yō ni karada o daiji ni shite (atsukatte) imasu ka.
How do you take care of your body?

52 タバコを吸うのは体（健康）に良くないです。
Tabako o sū no wa karada (kenkō) ni yokunai desu.
Smoking is bad for your health.

53 飲み過ぎ食べ過ぎに注意してください。
Tabesugi nomisugi ni chūi shite kudasai.
Be careful not to eat and drink too much.

54 お菓子や甘いものを食べ過ぎないでください。
Okashi ya amai mono o tabesuginaide kudasai.
Don't eat too many sweets and snacks.

55 健康でいるために、毎日運動するほうがいいです。
Kenkō de iru tame ni, mainichi undō suru hō ga ii desu.
To stay healthy, you should exercise every day.

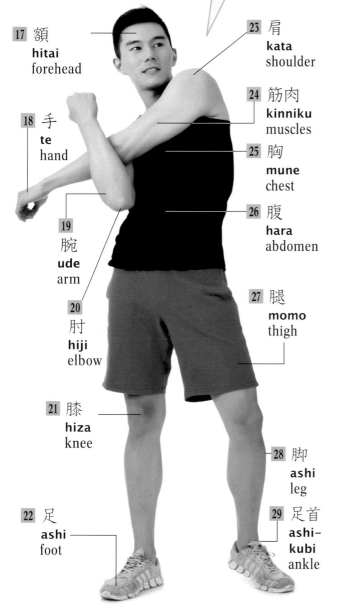

17 額
hitai
forehead

18 手
te
hand

19 腕
ude
arm

20 肘
hiji
elbow

21 膝
hiza
knee

22 足
ashi
foot

23 肩
kata
shoulder

24 筋肉
kinniku
muscles

25 胸
mune
chest

26 腹
hara
abdomen

27 腿
momo
thigh

28 脚
ashi
leg

29 足首
ashi-kubi
ankle

Additional Vocabulary

36 臓器
zōki
organs

37 消化器系
shōkakikei
digestive system

38 呼吸器系
kokyūkikei
respiratory system

39 神経系
shinkeikei
nervous system

40 骨格
kokkaku
skeletal system

41 皮膚
hifu
skin

42 血; 血液
chi; ketsueki
blood

43 血管
kekkan
vessels

44 骨
hone
bone

45 動脈
dōmyaku
artery

46 静脈
jōmyaku
vein

47 健康
kenkō
health

48 病気
byōki
illness

49 胃
i
stomach

30 脳
nō
brain

31 肺
hai
lungs

32 心臓
shinzō
heart

33 腎臓
jinzō
kidneys

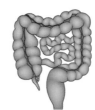

34 腸
chō
intestines

35 肝臓
kanzō
liver

数を数える

Kazu o kazoeru

Counting and Numbers

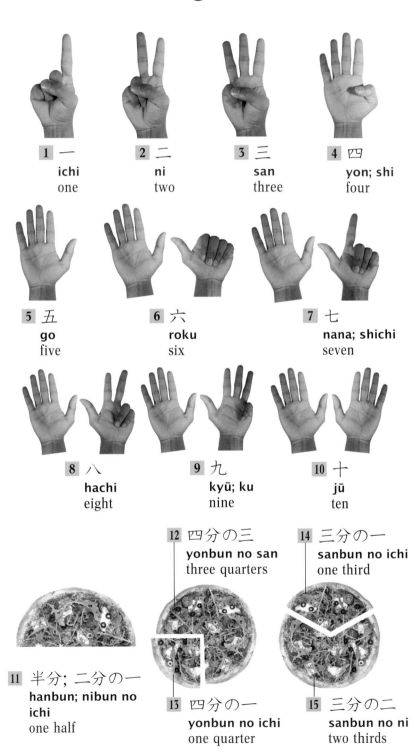

1 一	2 二	3 三	4 四
ichi	ni	san	yon; shi
one	two	three	four

5 五	6 六	7 七
go	roku	nana; shichi
five	six	seven

8 八	9 九	10 十
hachi	kyū; ku	jū
eight	nine	ten

12 四分の三
yonbun no san
three quarters

14 三分の一
sanbun no ichi
one third

11 半分; 二分の一
hanbun; nibun no ichi
one half

13 四分の一
yonbun no ichi
one quarter

15 三分の二
sanbun no ni
two thirds

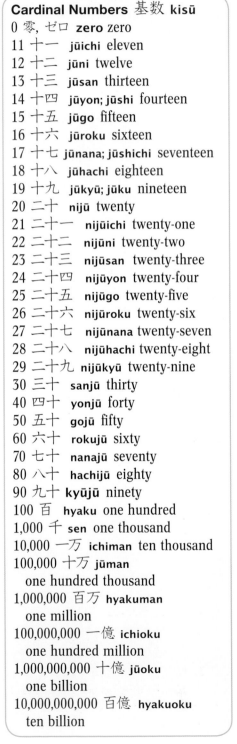

Cardinal Numbers 基数 **kisū**

0 零, ゼロ **zero** zero
11 十一 **jūichi** eleven
12 十二 **jūni** twelve
13 十三 **jūsan** thirteen
14 十四 **jūyon; jūshi** fourteen
15 十五 **jūgo** fifteen
16 十六 **jūroku** sixteen
17 十七 **jūnana; jūshichi** seventeen
18 十八 **jūhachi** eighteen
19 十九 **jūkyū; jūku** nineteen
20 二十 **nijū** twenty
21 二十一 **nijūichi** twenty-one
22 二十二 **nijūni** twenty-two
23 二十三 **nijūsan** twenty-three
24 二十四 **nijūyon** twenty-four
25 二十五 **nijūgo** twenty-five
26 二十六 **nijūroku** twenty-six
27 二十七 **nijūnana** twenty-seven
28 二十八 **nijūhachi** twenty-eight
29 二十九 **nijūkyū** twenty-nine
30 三十 **sanjū** thirty
40 四十 **yonjū** forty
50 五十 **gojū** fifty
60 六十 **rokujū** sixty
70 七十 **nanajū** seventy
80 八十 **hachijū** eighty
90 九十 **kyūjū** ninety
100 百 **hyaku** one hundred
1,000 千 **sen** one thousand
10,000 一万 **ichiman** ten thousand
100,000 十万 **jūman**
 one hundred thousand
1,000,000 百万 **hyakuman**
 one million
100,000,000 一億 **ichioku**
 one hundred million
1,000,000,000 十億 **jūoku**
 one billion
10,000,000,000 百億 **hyakuoku**
 ten billion

16 計算機; 電卓
keisanki; dentaku
calculator

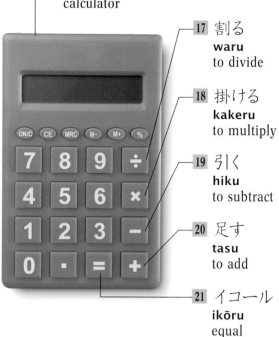

17 割る
waru
to divide

18 掛ける
kakeru
to multiply

19 引く
hiku
to subtract

20 足す
tasu
to add

21 イコール
ikōru
equal

Additional Vocabulary

22 足し算
tashizan
addition

23 引き算
hikizan
subtraction

24 掛け算
kakezan
multiplication

25 割り算
warizan
division

26 偶数
gūsū
even numbers

27 奇数
kisū
odd numbers

28 数; 番号
kazu; bangō
numbers

29 桁数
ketasū
digits; number

Ordinal Numbers 序数 **josū**
Note: To form an ordinal number, just add the word 第 **dai** in front of the number. For example:
1st 第一 **dai-ichi** first
2nd 第二 **dai-ni** second
3rd 第三 **dai-san** third
4th 第四 **dai-yon** fourth
5th 第五 **dai-go** fifth
6th 第六 **dai-roku** sixth
7th 第七 **dai-nana** seventh
8th 第八 **dai-hachi** eighth
9th 第九 **dai-kyū** ninth
10th 第十 **dai-jū** tenth
11th 第十一 **dai-jūichi** eleventh
12th 第十二 **dai-jūni** twelfth
13th 第十三 **dai-jūsan** thirteenth
20th 第二十 **dai-nijū** twentieth
30th 第三十 **dai-sanjū** thirtieth
40th 第四十 **dai-yonjū** fourtieth
50th 第五十 **dai-gojū** fiftieth
60th 第六十 **dai-rokujū** sixtieth
70th 第七十 **dai-nanajū** seventieth
80th 第八十 **dai-hachijū** eightieth
90th 第九十 **dai-kyūjū** ninetieth
100th 第百 **dai-hyaku** one-hundredth
1,000th 第千 **dai-sen** one-thousandth

30 二足す四は六です。
Ni tasu yon wa roku desu.
Two plus four equals six.

31 十一引く五は六です。
Jūichi hiku go wa roku desu.
Eleven minus five equals six.

32 十掛ける十二は百二十です。
Jū kakeru jūni wa hyakunijū desu.
Ten times twelve equals one hundred and twenty.

33 四十二割る八は五と四分の一です。
Yonjūni waru hachi wa go to yonbun no ichi desu.
Forty-two divided by eight equals five and a quarter.

6 日常生活
Nichijō seikatsu
Daily Activities

1 聞く
kiku
to listen

2 見る
miru
to look; see

3 泣く
naku
to cry

4 笑う
warau
to laugh

5 立つ
tatsu
to stand

6 座る
suwaru
to sit

Additional Vocabulary

18 音
oto
sound

19 質問する
shitsumon suru
to ask

20 遊ぶ
asobu
to play

21 呼吸する
kokyū suru
to breathe

22 答える
kotaeru
to answer

23 見える
mieru
to catch sight of

24 学校へ行く
gakkō e iku
to go to school

25 放課後
hōkago
after school

26 仕事へ行く；
仕事から帰る
**shigoto e iku;
shigoto kara kaeru**
to go to work;
to get off work

27 料理する
ryōri suru
to cook; to prepare a
meal

28 シャワーを
浴びる
shawā o abiru
to take a shower

29 髪を洗う
kami o arau
to wash my hair

30 くつろぐ
kutsurogu
to relax

31 朝ご飯を食べる
asagohan o taberu
to have breakfast

32 昼ご飯を食べる
hirugohan o taberu
to have lunch

33 晩ご飯を食べる
bangohan o taberu
to have dinner

34 暇
hima
leisure

35 勉強時間
benkyō jikan
study time

36 家事をする
kaji o suru
to do household
chores

37 平日
heijitsu
weekday

38 週末
shūmatsu
weekend

39 怒る
okoru; ikaru
to get angry

40 解決する
kaiketsu suru
to resolve

41 要求する
yōkyū suru
to request

42 喜んで
yorokonde
to be willing (to do
something)

43 賛成する
sansei suru
to agree

44 私は毎日八時間の睡眠が必要です。
Watashi wa mainichi hachi-jikan no suimin ga hitsuyō desu.
I need eight hours of sleep every day.

7 寝る
neru
to sleep

8 テレビを見る
terebi o miru
to watch TV

9 書く
kaku
to write

10 起きる
okiru
to wake up

11 歯を磨く
ha o migaku
to brush teeth

12 話す
hanasu
to talk

13 伝える
tsutaeru
to speak

14 皆で食事をする
Minna de shokuji o suru
Everybody eats together

15 引っ越す
hikkosu
to move

16 手伝う
tetsudau
to help

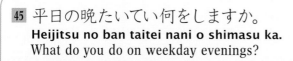

45 平日の晩たいてい何をしますか。
Heijitsu no ban taitei nani o shimasu ka.
What do you do on weekday evenings?

46 週末何をしますか。
Shūmatsu nani o shimasu ka.
What do you do on weekends?

47 毎日朝起きていつも何をしますか。
Mainichi asa okite itsumo nani o shimasu ka.
What is the first thing you do every morning?

48 私はシャワーを浴びて、歯を磨きます。
Watashi wa shawā o abite, ha o migakimasu.
I take a shower and brush my teeth.

17 犬を散歩させる
inu o sanpo saseru
to walk the dog

21

7 色と形
Iro to katachi
Colors and Shapes

1 色
iro
colors

2 赤
aka
red

3 白
shiro
white

4 黒
kuro
black

5 黄色
kiiro
yellow

6 青
ao
blue

7 緑
midori
green

8 紫
murasaki
purple

9 茶色
chairo
brown

10 灰色
haiiro
gray

11 オレンジ
orenji
orange

12 ピンク
pinku
pink

13 金色
kin'iro
gold

14 銀色
gin'iro
silver

15 濃い
koi
dark color

16 薄い
usui
light color

44 好きな色は何ですか。
Suki na iro wa nan desu ka.
What is your favorite color?

45 私は赤が好きです。
Watashi wa aka ga suki desu.
My favorite color is red.

17 虹
niji
a rainbow

18 四角形
shikakkei
a rectangle

19 円形
enkei
a circle

20 八角形
hakkakkei
an octagon

21 五角形
gokakkei
a pentagon

22 正方形
seihōkei
a square

23 ハート型
hātogata
a heart

24 だ円形
daenkei
an oval

25 星型
hoshigata
a star

26 三角形
sankakkei
a triangle

27 六角形
rokkakkei
a hexagon

28 ひし形
hishigata
a diamond

29 洋服のサイズ
yōfuku no saizu
clothing size

30 エックス
エスサイズ
ekkusu-esu saizu
XS size

31 エスサイズ
esu saizu
S size

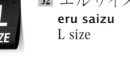

32 エルサイズ
eru saizu
L size

33 エックスエルサイズ
ekkusu-eru saizu
XL size

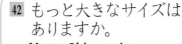

34 エムサイズ
emu saizu
M size

35 大きい
ōkii
large

36 中ぐらい
chūgurai
medium

37 小さい
chiisai
small

42 もっと大きなサイズは
ありますか。
**Motto ōkina saizu wa
arimasu ka.**
Do you have a larger size?

43 違う色はありますか。
Chigau iro wa arimasu ka.
Do you have this in other colors?

Additional Vocabulary

38 形
katachi
shape

39 大きさ;
サイズ
ōkisa; saizu
size

40 もっと
大きい
motto ōkii
larger

41 もっと
小さい
motto chiisai
smaller

反対語
Hantaigo
8
Opposites

1 上 ↔ 下
ue **shita**
up down

2 受ける ↔ あげる
ukeru **ageru**
receive give

3 たくさん ↔ 少し
takusan **sukoshi**
many few

5 背が高い ↔ 背が低い
se ga takai **se ga hikui**
tall short

6 出る ↔ 入る
deru **hairu**
exit enter

4 古い ↔ 新しい
furui **atarashii**
old new

7 良い ↔ 悪い
yoi **warui**
good bad

8 忙しい ↔ 暇
isogashii **hima**
busy idle

9 長い ↔ 短い
nagai **mijikai**
long short

10 年をとっています ↔ 若い
toshi o totte imasu **wakai**
old young

11 大きい ↔ 小さい
ōkii **chiisai**
big small

12 開ける ↔ 閉める
akeru **shimeru**
to open to close

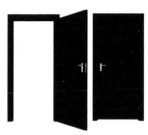

13 太っています ↔ 痩せています
futotte imasu **yasete imasu**
fat thin

14 着る ↔ 脱ぐ
kiru **nugu**
to put on to take off

15 難しい ↔ 優しい
muzukashii **yasashii**
difficult easy

16 ある ↔ ない
aru **nai**
to have not to have

17 来る ↔ 行く
kuru **iku**
to come to go

18 はい ↔ いいえ
hai **iie**
yes no

19 着く ↔ 出かける
tsuku **dekakeru**
to arrive to leave

20 中 ↔ 外
naka **soto**
inside outside

21 前 ↔ 後ろ
mae **ushiro**
in front behind

24 始まる ↔ 終わる
hajimaru **owaru**
to begin to end

25 近い ↔ 遠い
chikai **tōi**
near far

26 違う ↔ 正しい
chigau **tadashii**
wrong right

27 本物 ↔ 偽物
hon-mono **nise-mono**
real fake

28 速い ↔ 遅い
hayai **osoi**
fast slow

29 高い ↔ 低い
takai **hikui**
high low

30 借りる ↔ 貸す
kariru **kasu**
to borrow to lend

31 悲しい ↔ 嬉しい
kanashii **ureshii**
sad happy

22 お腹がいっぱいです ↔ お腹が空いています
onaka ga ippai desu **onaka ga suite imasu**
(stomach is) full hungry

23 覚える ↔ 忘れる
oboeru **wasureru**
to remember to forget

32 反対語を勉強することは外国語を習う良い方法です。
Hantaigo o benkyō suru koto wa gaikokugo o narau yoi hōhō desu.
Studying antonyms is a great way to learn a foreign language.

33 反対語は反対の意味を持つ二つの言葉です。
Hantaigo wa hantai no imi o motsu futatsu no kotoba desu.
Antonyms are a pair of words with the opposite meaning.

25

お金について話す

Okane ni tsuite hanasu

9 | Talking about Money

1 円
en
yen; Japanese currency

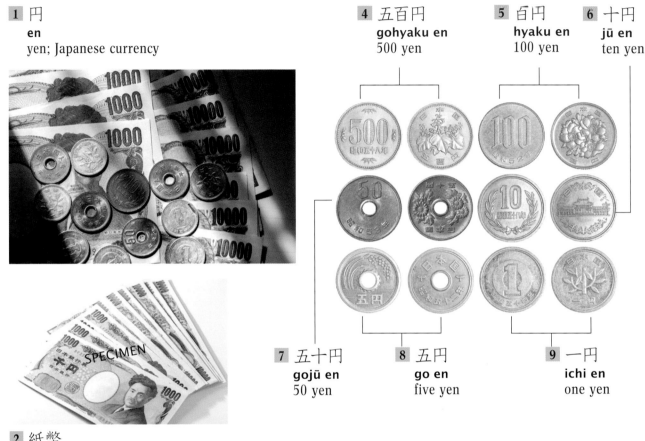

4 五百円
gohyaku en
500 yen

5 百円
hyaku en
100 yen

6 十円
jū en
ten yen

7 五十円
gojū en
50 yen

8 五円
go en
five yen

9 一円
ichi en
one yen

2 紙幣
shihei
paper money

3 硬貨
kōka
coins

10 一万円
ichiman en
10,000 yen

11 五千円
gosen en
5,000 yen

12 千円
sen en
1,000 yen

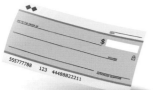

13 小切手
kogitte
check

14 小銭
kozeni
small change

15 クレジットカード
kurejitto kādo
credit card

16 貯金
chokin
savings

17 為替
kawase
currency exchange

18 引き出す
hikidasu
to withdraw money

Additional Vocabulary

19 お金
okane
coin; money

20 値段
nedan
price

21 割引
waribiki
discount

22 安い
yasui
cheap

23 高い
takai
expensive

24 利子
rishi
interest

25 ローン
rōn
loan; credit

26 借金
shakkin
debt

27 預金
yokin
bank deposit

28 口座番号
kōza bangō
account number

29 領収書; レシート
ryōshūsho; reshiito
receipt

30 掛け金
kakekin
installment
(payment)

31 税金
zeikin
tax

32 現金
genkin
cash

33 これはいくらですか。
Kore wa ikura desu ka.
How much does this cost?

34 二千四百九十五円です。
Nisen yonhyaku kyūjū go en desu.
Two thousand four hundred and
ninety-five yen (JPY ¥2,495).

35 もっと安くできませんか。
Motto yasuku dekimasen ka.
Can you give a discount?

36 十パーセントの割引
はいかがですか。
**Juppāsento no waribiki
wa ikaga desu ka.**
OK, 10% discount.

27

10 買い物に行く
Kaimono ni iku
Going Shopping

1 買う
kau
to buy

43 いくらですか。
Ikura desu ka.
How much is it?

2 売る
uru
to sell

3 買い物をする
kaimono o suru
to shop

4 買い物袋
kaimono-bukuro
shopping bag

5 腕時計
ude dokei
wrist watch

6 服
fuku
clothes

7 ブラウス
burausu
blouse

11 メガネ
megane
glasses; spectacles

14 シャツ
shatsu
shirt

8 スカート
sukāto
skirt

9 ジーンズ
jiinzu
jeans

10 ズボン
zubon
trousers

12 靴下
kutsushita
socks

13 靴
kutsu
shoes

15 ネクタイ
nekutai
necktie

16 帽子
bōshi
hat

Some useful shopping expressions:

46 一番近い商店街はどこですか。
Ichiban chikai shōtengai wa doko desu ka.
Where is the nearest shopping center?

47 これを試着しても良いですか。
Kore o shichaku shitemo yoi desu ka.
Can I try it on?

48 試着室はどこですか。
Shichakushitsu wa doko desu ka.
Where is the fitting room?

49 それは高すぎます。
Sore wa takasugimasu.
That's too expensive!

50 これにします。
Kore ni shimasu.
I'll take it.

51 クレジットカードで良いですか。
Kurejitto kādo de yoi desu ka.
Do you accept credit cards?

52 現金で払います。
Genkin de haraimasu.
I'll pay in cash.

53 領収書をお願いします。
Ryōshūsho o onegai shimasu.
Could I have a receipt?

17 化粧品
keshōhin
cosmetics

18 おもちゃ
omocha
toys

19 ベルト
beruto
belt

20 スカーフ
sukāfu
scarf

Additional Vocabulary

21 ブラックフライデー
burakku furaidē
Black Friday

22 店
mise
shop

23 デパート
depāto
department store

24 ブティック
butikku
boutique

25 店員
ten'in
shop staff

26 レジ
reji
cashier

27 宅配
takuhai
home delivery

28 値段を比べる
nedan o kuraberu
to compare prices

29 通販
tsūhan
online shopping

30 クレジットカード
kurejitto kādo
credit card

31 同じ
onaji
the same as

32 全部で
zenbu de
altogether

33 必ず
kanarazu
certainly

34 一般
ippan
generally

35 もっと
motto
more; even more

36 決定
kettei
decision

37 他
hoka
other

38 持って来る
mottekuru
to bring

39 もの
mono
things

40 会計
kaikei
bill; invoice

41 免税
menzei
tax free

42 払い戻し
haraimodoshi
refund

44 これは税込みですか。
Kore wa zeikomi desu ka.
Does this include tax?

45 後で税金を返金してもらえますか。
Ato de zeikin o henkin shite moraemasu ka.
Can I refund the tax later?

11 街の生活
Machi no seikatsu
Life in the City

1 空港
kūkō
airport

2 ホテル
hoteru
hotel

3 店 **4** 道
mise **michi**
shop street

5 スーパー
sūpā
supermarket

6 ガソリンスタンド
gasorin sutando
gas station;
petrol station

7 銀行
ginkō
bank

8 会館
kaikan
conference center

9 駅
eki
train station

10 博物館
hakubutsukan
museum

11 都会; 街
tokai; machi
city

12 超高層ビル
chōkōsō biru
skyscraper

13 アパート
apāto
apartment building

14 美術館
bijutsukan
art museum

15 スタジアム
sutajiamu
stadium

16 郵便局
yūbinkyoku
post office

17 警察署
keisatsusho
police station

18 高速道路
kōsoku dōro
expressway

19 フィットネスジム
fittonesu jimu
gym

20 ホテル
hoteru
hotel

21 映画館
eigakan
movie theater

22 ショッピングモール
shoppingu mōru
shopping center; mall

23 中心部
chūshinbu
downtown

24 ビジネス街
bijinesugai
business district

25 郊外
kōgai
suburb

26 家
ie
house

27 橋
hashi
bridge

28 歩道
hodō
sidewalk

29 隣人
rinjin
neighbor

30 街角
machikado
street corner

31 記念碑
kinenhi
monument

32 教会
kyōkai
church

33 交通
kōtsū
traffic

34 歩行者
hokōsha
pedestrian

35 寺
tera
temple

36 神社
jinja
Shinto shrine

37 信号
shingō
traffic lights

38 道路
dōro
road

39 お住まいは街中ですか、郊外ですか。
Osumai wa machinaka desu ka, kōgai desu ka.
Do you live in the city? Or in the suburb?

40 どうやって仕事へ通ってますか。
Dōyatte shigoto e kayotte imasu ka.
How do you go to work?

41 都心部から空港までは、どれくらいかかりますか。
Toshinbu kara kūkō made wa, dorekurai kakarimasu ka.
How far is the city center from the airport?

42 田中さんは、都市部に住みたがっています。
Tanaka-san wa, toshibu ni sumitagatte imasu.
Miss Tanaka wants to live in the city.

12 街で
Machi de
Around Town

1 車
kuruma
car

2 タクシー
takushii
taxi

3 運転手
untenshu
driver

4 飛行機
hikōki
airplane

5 トラック
torakku
truck

6 ゴミ収集車
gomi shūshūsha
garbage truck

7 配送トラック
haisō torakku
delivery van

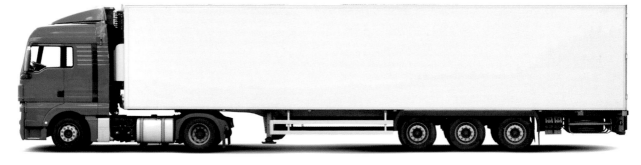

8 新幹線
shinkansen
bullet train

9 バイク;
オートバイ
baiku; ōtobai
motorcycle

10 スポーツカー
supōtsukā
sports car

13 バス停
basutei
bus stop

11 地下鉄
chikatetsu
subway

12 バス
basu
public bus

14 客船
kyakusen
ship; boat

Additional Vocabulary

15 電車
densha
train

16 消防車
shōbōsha
fire engine

17 路面電車
romen densha
tram

18 自転車
jitensha
bicycle

19 乗客
jōkyaku
passenger

20 バスに乗る
basu ni noru
to catch a bus

21 バスで
basu de
by bus; to take
a bus

22 電車に乗る
densha ni noru
to ride a train

23 電車で
densha de
by train; to take
a train

24 車を運転する
kuruma o unten suru
to drive a car

25 自転車に乗る
jitensha ni noru
to ride a bike

26 もっとゆっくり
motto yukkuri
slow down

27 もっと速く
motto hayaku
go faster

28 左/右に曲がって
ください
**hidari/migi ni
magatte kudasai**
turn left/turn right

29 まっすぐ行って
ください
massugu itte kudasai
go straight

30 電車時刻表
densha jikokuhyō
train schedule

31 切符売り場
kippu uriba
ticket counter

32 バス路線
basu rosen
bus route

33 馬車
basha
horse carriage

34 タクシーを呼ぶ
takushii o yobu
to call a taxi

35 ウーバー
ūbā
Uber

36 街の中心部には、どうやって行けばいいですか。
Machi no chūshinbu ni wa, dōyatte ikeba ii desu ka.
What is the best way to get downtown?

37 バスで行けます。タクシー、地下鉄でも行けます。
Basu de ikemasu. Takushii, chikatetsu demo ikemasu.
By bus, by taxi or take the subway.

38 地下鉄の駅へはどう行けばいいですか。
Chikatetsu no eki e wa dō ikeba ii desu ka.
How do I get to the subway station?

13 道を尋ねる
Michi o tazuneru
Asking Directions

1 どこ
doko
where?

Compass

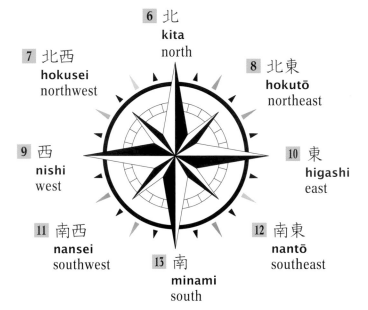

6 北
kita
north

7 北西
hokusei
northwest

8 北東
hokutō
northeast

9 西
nishi
west

10 東
higashi
east

11 南西
nansei
southwest

12 南東
nantō
southeast

13 南
minami
south

14 前
mae
in front

15 後ろ
ushiro
behind

2 ここ
koko
here

3 そこ；あそこ
soko; asoko
there; over there

4 上
ue
above

5 下
shita
below

Some common phrases for asking and giving directions:

16 道をたずねる
michi o tazuneru
to ask directions

17 道に迷いました。たすけてもらえますか。
Michi ni mayoimashita. Tasukete moraemasu ka.
I'm lost. Can you help me?

18 これは…への道ですか。
Kore wa ... e no michi desu ka.
Is this the way to … ?

19 どのくらいありますか。
Dono kurai arimasu ka.
How far is it?

20 地図で教えてもらえますか。
Chizu de oshiete moraemasu ka.
Can you show me on the map?

21 道を教える
michi o oshieru
to give directions

22 すみません。よくわかりません。
Sumimasen. Yoku wakarimasen.
I'm sorry, I don't know.

23 こちらが道です。
Kochira ga michi desu.
It's this way.

24 それがあの道です。
Sore ga ano michi desu.
It's that way.

25 左側/右側にあります。
Hidarigawa/migigawa ni arimasu.
It's on the left/right.

26 …の隣にあります。
... no tonari ni arimasu.
It's next to … .

27 右側
migigawa
right side

28 間
aida
middle; center

29 左側
hidarigawa
left side

30 左へ曲がる
hidari e magaru
to turn left

31 直進
chokushin
to go straight

32 右へ曲がる
migi e magaru
to turn right

33 外側
soto-gawa
outside

34 内側
uchigawa
inside

35 道に迷う
michi ni mayou
to be lost

36 方向
hōkō
direction

37 距離
kyori
distance

38 キロ
kiro
kilometer

39 マイル
mairu
mile

40 メートル
mētoru
meter

41 フィート
fiito
foot

42 近い
chikai
near

43 遠い
tōi
far

44 向かい側
mukaigawa
opposite

45 東部
tōbu
the east

46 南部
nanbu
the south

47 西部
seibu
the west

48 北部
hokubu
the north

49 隣
tonari
next; side

50 そば
soba
nearby

51 場所
basho
place

52 片方
katahō
one side

53 教える
oshieru
to tell

54 通る
tōru
to go through

55 出かける
dekakeru
to leave

56 どのくらい
dono kurai
how much
(time/distance)

57 もうすぐ
mōsugu
soon; very soon

58 させる
saseru
to allow; to cause

59 すでに
sude ni
already

60 思う
omou
to think

61 考える
kangaeru
to consider

62 助ける
tasukeru
to help

63 心配する
shinpai suru
to feel anxious

天気について話す

Tenki ni tsuite hanasu

14 Telling about the Weather

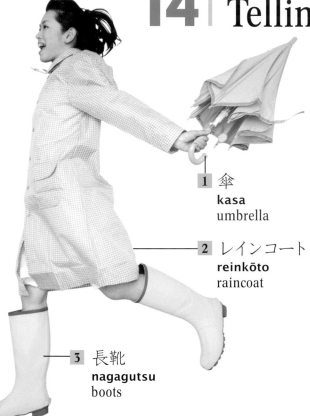

1 傘
kasa
umbrella

2 レインコート
reinkōto
raincoat

3 長靴
nagagutsu
boots

4 晴れ
hare
clear (sky)

5 晴れた日
hareta hi
clear day

6 曇り
kumori
overcast

7 曇った日
kumotta hi
cloudy day

8 風
kaze
wind

9 風が強い
kaze ga tsuyoi
windy

10 雨
ame
rain

11 雨降り
amefuri
raining

12 稲妻
inazuma
lightning

13 雷
kaminari
thunder

14 嵐
arashi
thunderstorm

15 雪
yuki
snow

16 雪が降る
yuki ga furu
to snow

17 台風
taifū
typhoon

---

39 今日は良い天気です。明日は雨だそうです。
Kyō wa yoi tenki desu. Ashita wa ame da sō desu.
It's a beautiful day today. Tomorrow will be rainy.

40 今日は暑すぎます。明日は涼しくなります。
Kyō wa atsusugi masu. Ashita wa suzushikunari masu.
It is too hot today. Tomorrow will be cooler.

18 コート
kōto
coat or jacket

19 セーター
sētā
sweater

Additional Vocabulary

32 天気
tenki
weather

33 天気予報
tenki yohō
weather forecast

34 良い天気
yoi tenki
good weather

35 悪い天気
warui tenki
bad weather

36 晴れた天気
hareta tenki
sunny weather

37 大気汚染
taiki osen
air pollution

38 ハリケーン
harikēn
hurricane

20 暑い
atsui
hot

21 暑い日
atsui hi
hot day

22 寒い
samui
cold

23 寒い日
samui hi
cold day

24 雲
kumo
cloud

25 霧
kiri
fog

26 太陽
taiyō
sun

27 月
tsuki
moon

28 暴風雨
bōfūu
rainstorm

29 霰
arare
hail

30 帽子
bōshi
hat

31 手袋
tebukuro
gloves

37

時間について話す
Jikan ni tsuite hanasu

15 | Telling Time

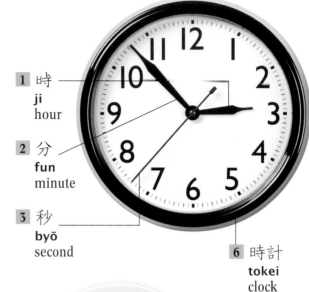

1 時
ji
hour

2 分
fun
minute

3 秒
byō
second

6 時計
tokei
clock

4 六時
rokuji
6 o'clock

5 六時五分
rokuji gofun
five minutes past six

8 六時十五分
rokuji jūgofun
fifteen minutes past six;
a quarter past six

9 六時半
rokuji han
half past six

7 十五分
jūgofun
quarter
(hour)

10 六時四十五分;
七時十五分前
rokuji yonjūgofun;
shichiji jūgofun mae
fifteen minutes to seven;
a quarter to seven

11 六時五十五分;
七時五分前
rokuji gojūgofun;
shichiji gofun mae
five minutes
to seven

37 今何時ですか。
Ima nanji desu ka.
What's the time?

38 八時半です。
Hachiji han desu.
Half past eight.

39 すみません。遅くなりました。
Sumimasen. Osokunarimashita.
Sorry, I'm late.

40 いいえ、大丈夫です。
Iie, daijōbu desu.
It's OK.

17 今
ima
now

18 過去
kako
(in the) past

19 よく
yoku
frequently

20 時間
jikan
time

21 早朝
sōchō
early morning

22 午前
gozen
in the morning;
a.m.

23 正午
shōgo
noon

24 午後
gogo
in the afternoon;
p.m.

25 真夜中
mayonaka
midnight

26 時間を守る
jikan o mamoru
punctual

27 早い
hayai
early

28 遅い
osoi
late

29 今度
kondo
next time

30 後で
ato de
later

31 前
mae
before

32 間
aida
between; among

33 一瞬
isshun
a brief moment

34 じきに
jiki ni
in a moment

35 突然
totsuzen
suddenly

36 ようやく
yōyaku
finally

12 目覚し時計
mezamashi-dokei
alarm clock

13 ストップウォッチ
sutoppuwotchi
stopwatch

14 スマートウォッチ
sumātowotchi
smartwatch

15 腕時計
ude dokei
wrist watch

41 三時に会いましょう。
Sanji ni aimashō.
Let's meet at 3 p.m.

16 夜
yoru
night

16

年と日付
Toshi to hizuke
Years and Dates

4 年
nen; toshi
year

1 カレンダー
karendā
calendar

2 月
gatsu;
getsu
month

3 曜日
yōbi
a day of
the week

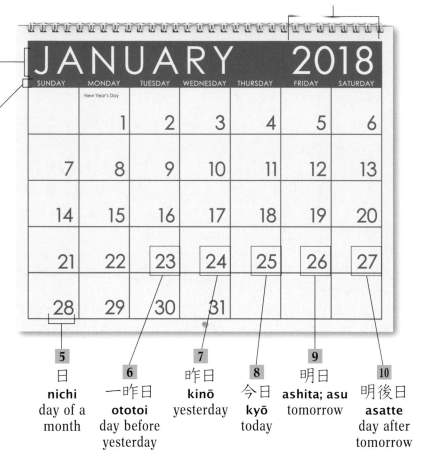

JANUARY 2018

SUNDAY	MONDAY	TUESDAY	WEDNESDAY	THURSDAY	FRIDAY	SATURDAY
	1 New Year's Day	2	3	4	5	6
7	8	9	10	11	12	13
14	15	16	17	18	19	20
21	22	23	24	25	26	27
28	29	30	31			

11 日曜日 **Nichiyōbi** Sunday
12 月曜日 **Getsuyōbi** Monday
13 火曜日 **Kayōbi** Tuesday
14 水曜日 **Suiyōbi** Wednesday
15 木曜日 **Mokuyōbi** Thursday
16 金曜日 **Kin'yōbi** Friday
17 土曜日 **Doyōbi** Saturday

5
日
nichi
day of a
month

6
一昨日
ototoi
day before
yesterday

7
昨日
kinō
yesterday

8
今日
kyō
today

9
明日
ashita; asu
tomorrow

10
明後日
asatte
day after
tomorrow

46 私は日記を書くのが好きです。
Watashi wa nikki o kaku
no ga suki desu.
I like to keep a diary.

47 今日は一月二十五日木曜日です。
Kyō wa ichigatsu nijūgonichi mokuyōbi desu.
Today is Thursday, January 25.

48 昨日は一月二十四日水曜日でした。
Kinō wa ichigatsu nijūyokka suiyōbi deshita.
Yesterday was Wednesday, January 24.

49 明日は一月二十六日金曜日です。
Ashita wa ichigatsu nijūrokunichi kin'yōbi desu.
Tomorrow will be Friday, January 26.

How to express years, months, and dates in Japanese: In Japanese, years are expressed similarly to English, except they are followed by the character 年 (**nen**), meaning "year." For example,

2020 = 二千二十年 **nisen nijū-nen**   1964 = 千九百六十四年 **sen kyūhyaku rokujū yo-nen**
1776 = 千七百七十六年 **sen nanahyaku nanajū roku-nen**

The 12 months of the year in Japanese are:

18 January 一月 **ichigatsu**	22 May 五月 **gogatsu**	26 September 九月 **kugatsu**	
19 February 二月 **nigatsu**	23 June 六月 **rokugatsu**	27 October 十月 **jūgatsu**	
20 March 三月 **sangatsu**	24 July 七月 **shichigatsu**	28 November 十一月 **jūichigatsu**	
21 April 四月 **shigatsu**	25 August 八月 **hachigatsu**	29 December 十二月 **jūnigatsu**	

Dates are expressed as the date, plus 日 (**nichi**), meaning day of the month, for dates between 11th and 31st. Dates between 1st and 10th are exceptions, as are 14th, 20th and 24th. See below,

1st	一日	**tsuitachi**	11th	十一日	**jūichinichi**	21st	二十一日	**nijūichinichi**
2nd	二日	**futsuka**	12th	十二日	**jūninichi**	22nd	二十二日	**nijūninichi**
3rd	三日	**mikka**	13th	十三日	**jūsannichi**	23rd	二十三日	**nijūsannichi**
4th	四日	**yokka**	14th	十四日	**jūyokka**	24th	二十四日	**nijūyokka**
5th	五日	**itsuka**	15th	十五日	**jūgonichi**			
6th	六日	**muika**	16th	十六日	**jūrokunichi**			
7th	七日	**nanoka**	17th	十七日	**jūshichinichi**	31st	三十一日	**sanjūichinichi**
8th	八日	**yōka**	18th	十八日	**jūhachinichi**			
9th	九日	**kokonoka**	19th	十九日	**jūkunichi**			
10th	十日	**tōka**	20th	二十日	**hatsuka**			

Dates are expressed with the month first, followed by the date of the month. For example,

January 1st (New Years Day) = 一月一日 **ichigatsu tsuitachi**
May 5th (Children's Day) = 五月五日 **gogatsu itsuka**
July 7th (Star Festival) = 七月七日 **shichigatsu nanoka**

50 お誕生日はいつですか。
Otanjōbi wa itsu desu ka.
When is your birthday?

51 私の誕生日は一月三十一日です。
Watashi no tanjōbi wa ichigatsu sanjūichinichi desu.
My birthday is on January 31.

Additional Vocabulary

30 去年 **kyonen** last year	34 再来年 **sarainen** the year after next	38 十年 **jūnen** decade (10 years)	42 先月 **sengetsu** last month
31 一昨年 **ototoshi** the year before last	35 週間 **shūkan** week	39 世紀 **seiki** century (100 years)	43 来週 **raishū** next week
32 今年 **kotoshi** this year	36 歳 **sai; toshi** years (of age)	40 千年 **sennen** millennium (1000 years)	44 来月 **raigetsu** next month
33 来年 **rainen** next year	37 閏年 **urūdoshi** leap year	41 先週 **senshū** last week	45 日記 **nikki** diary

四季
Shiki
17 Four Seasons

1 春
haru
spring

2 夏
natsu
summer

3 秋
aki
autumn; fall

4 冬
fuyu
winter

5 暖かい
atatakai
warm

6 そよ風
soyokaze
a gentle breeze

7 桃の花
momo no hana
peach blossoms

8 咲く
saku
to flower

9 小雨
kosame
to drizzle

10 日傘
higasa
sunshade; parasole

11 水遊び
mizuasobi
water play

12 雪だるまを作る
yukidaruma o tsukuru
to make a snowman

13 収穫
shūkaku
harvest

17 作物
sakumotsu
crops

The changing colors of the seasons.
季節ごとに変わる色 Kisetsu goto ni kawaru iro

春に咲く花	夏の緑	秋の紅葉	冬の雪
haru ni saku hana	**natsu no midori**	**aki no kōyō**	**fuyu no yuki**
spring blossoms	summer greenery	autumn foliage	winter snow

14 扇子
sensu
fan

15 雪合戦
yukigassen
snowball fights

16 日焼け止め
hiyakedome
sunblock lotion

Additional Vocabulary

18 四季
shiki
four seasons

19 前の
mae no
former

20 実は
jitsu wa
actually

21 私は海で水遊びするのが好きです。
Watashi wa umi de mizuasobi suru no ga suki desu.
I like to go to the beach and play in the water.

22 一年に季節はいくつありますか。
Ichinen ni kisetsu wa ikutsu arimasu ka.
How many seasons are there in a year?

23 一年に季節は四つあります。
Ichinen ni kisetsu wa yottsu arimasu.
There are four seasons in a year.

24 どの季節が好きですか。
Dono kisetsu ga suki desu ka.
Which season do you like best?

25 私は夏が一番好きです。
Watashi ha natsu ga ichiban suki desu.
My favorite season is summer.

18

祝日を祝う
Shukujitsu o iwau
Celebrating the Holidays

1 祝日; 祭日
shukujitsu; saijitsu
festival; holiday

2 新年
Shinnen
New Year

3 花火
hanabi
fireworks

4 成人の日
Seijin no hi
Coming of Age Day

5 節分
Setsubun
beginning of spring

6 子供の日
Kodomo no hi
Children's Day

7 七夕
Tanabata
Star Festival

8 体育の日
Taiiku no hi
Health and Sports Day

9 運動会
undōkai
sports day event

10 文化の日
Bunka no hi
Culture Day

11 お餅
omochi
sticky rice cake

12 和菓子
wagashi
Japanese traditional cakes

13 父の日
Chichi no hi
Father's Day

14 母の日
Haha no hi
Mother's Day

15 バレンタインデー
Barentain dē
Valentine's Day

16 チョコレート
chokorēto
chocolates

17 バラ
bara
roses

18 感謝祭
（勤労感謝の日）
Kanshasai
(Kinrō kansha no hi)
Thanksgiving

19 ハロウィーン
Harowiin
Halloween

20 復活祭
fukkatsusai
Easter

21 憲法記念日
Kenpō Kinenbi
Constitution Day

37 あけましておめでとうございます。
Akemashite omedetō gozaimasu.
Happy New Year!

38 一緒にお正月を祝いませんか。
Issho ni oshōgatsu o iwaimasen ka.
Please join us for the New Year celebrations.

Additional Vocabulary

25 誕生日
tanjōbi
birthday

26 誕生会へ行く
tanjōkai e iku
attend a birthday party

27 夏休み
natsuyasumi
summer vacation

28 冬休み
fuyuyasumi
winter vacation

29 記念日
kinenbi
anniversary

30 周年
shūnen
whole year; anniversary

31 ゴールデンウィーク
Gōruden wiiku
Golden Week

32 ホワイトデー
howaitodē
White Day

33 ひな祭り
Hinamatsuri
Doll Festival

34 天皇誕生日
Tennō tanjōbi
Emperor's
Birthday

35 お誕生日おめでとう！
Otanjōbi omedetō!
Happy birthday!

22 贈り物; プレゼント
okurimono; purezento
gift

36 メリークリスマス！
Merii kurisumasu!
Merry Christmas!

23 クリスマス
kurisumasu
Christmas

24 サンタクロース
santakurōsu
Santa Claus

学ぶのが好き

Manabu no ga suki

19 | I Love to Learn

1 試験; テスト
shiken; tesuto
exams

2 読む
yomu
to read

3 勉強する
benkyō suru
to learn; to study

4 数学
sūgaku
mathematics

5 体育
taiiku
physical education

6 答える
kotaeru
to answer

7 本
hon
book

8 ニュース
nyūsu
the news

9 新聞
shinbun
newspaper

10 雑誌
zasshi
magazine

12 手紙
tegami
letter

11 辞書
jisho
dictionary

13 ペン
pen
pen

14 消しゴム
keshigomu
eraser

15 マーカー
mākā
marker pen

16 鉛筆削り
enpitsu kezuri
pencil sharpener

17 物差し；定規
monosashi; jōgi
ruler

18 ノート
nōto
notebook

19 蛍光ペン
keikōpen
highlighter

20 鉛筆
enpitsu
pencil

21 ハサミ
hasami
scissors

Additional Vocabulary

22 級
kyū
grade; class

23 わかる
wakaru
to understand

24 練習する
renshū suru
to practice

25 復習する
fukushū suru
to review

26 問題
mondai
a question;
problem

27 宿題
shukudai
homework

28 文学
bungaku
literature

29 歴史
rekishi
history

30 単語
tango
word

31 物語
monogatari
story

32 課題
kadai
assignment

33 大好き
daisuki
love

34 幾何学
kikagaku
geometry

35 科学
kagaku
science

36 社会学
shakaigaku
sociology

37 経済学
keizaigaku
economics

38 代数
daisū
algebra

39 物理
butsuri
physics

40 化学
kagaku
chemistry

41 生物学
seibutsugaku
biology

42 微積分
bisekibun
calculus

43 地理
chiri
geography

44 テスト
tesuto
test

45 才能
sainō
talent; ability

46 真面目
majime
conscientious;
serious

47 水準
suijun
level (of
achievement)

48 上手になる
jōzu ni naru
to improve

49 上位
jōi
top rank

50 理解する
rikai suru
to understand

51 目的
mokuteki
purpose

53 一番好きな科目は何ですか。
Ichiban suki na kamoku wa nan desu ka.
What is your most favorite subject?

54 私は文学と歴史が好きです。
Watashi wa bungaku to rekishi ga suki desu.
I like literature and history.

52 私は本が
大好きです。
**Watashi wa hon
ga daisuki desu.**
I love books!

20 学校で
Gakkō de
At School

1 ホワイトボード
howaitobōdo
whiteboard

2 黒板
kokuban
blackboard

3 図書館
toshokan
library

4 教室
kyōshitsu
classroom

5 教える
oshieru
to teach

6 先生
sensei
teacher

7 コピー機
kopiiki
photocopier

8 コピーをとる
kopii o toru
to photocopy

9 手をあげる
te o ageru
to raise your hand

11 科学
kagaku
science

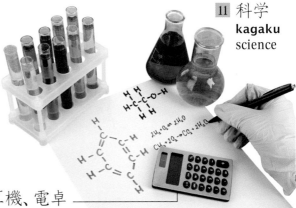

10 計算機、電卓
keisanki; dentaku
calculator

12 教授
kyōju
professor

13 講義室
kōgishitsu
lecture hall

14 生徒; 学生
seito; gakusei
student

15 同級生; クラスメート
dōkyūsei; kurasumēto
classmates

51 宿題を手伝ってあげましょうか。
Shukudai o tetsudatte agemashō ka.
Do you need help with your assignment?

16 学校
gakkō
school

17 校長
kōchō
principal

18 教師
kyōshi
teacher

19 講堂
kōdō
auditorium

20 コンピューターラボ
konpyūtārabo
computer lab

21 研究室
kenkyushitsu
laboratory

22 アルファベット
arufabetto
alphabet

23 成績
seiseki
grades

24 賢い
kashikoi
intelligent; clever

25 教科書
kyōkasho
textbook

26 ワークブック
wākubukku
workbook

27 私立学校
shiritsu gakkō
private school

28 公立学校
kōritsu gakkō
public school

29 幼稚園
yōchien
nursery school

30 学校へ行く
gakkō e iku
to attend school

31 小学校
shōgakkō
elementary school

32 中学校
chūgakkō
middle school

33 高校
kōkō
senior high school

34 大学
daigaku
university; college

35 大学一年生
daigaku ichinensei
freshman year in college

36 大学二年生
daigaku ninensei
sophomore year in college

37 大学三年生
daigaku sannensei
junior year in college

38 大学四年生
daigaku yonensei
senior year in college

39 塾
juku
cram school

40 専攻する
senkō suru
to major

41 題
dai
topic

42 必修
hisshū
compulsory

43 また
mata
also

44 優れる
sugureru
to exceed

45 卒業する
sotsugyō suru
to graduate

46 何年生ですか。
Nannensei desu ka.
What year are you?

47 大学二年生です。
Daigaku ninensei desu.
I'm a sophomore in college.

48 私の専攻は数学です。
Watashi no senkō wa sūgaku desu.
I'm majoring in math.

49 専攻はなんですか。
Senkō wa nan desu ka.
What is your major?

50 頭がいいですね。
Atama ga ii desu ne!
You must be very smart!

日本語を学ぶ
Nihongo o manabu

21 | Learning Japanese

1 日本語の発音はむずかしくないです。
Nihongo no hatsuon wa muzukashikunai desu.
Japanese is not a difficult language to pronounce.

2 でも、書くのは、時間がかかるでしょう。
Demo, kaku no wa, jikan ga kakaru deshō.
But, the writing system takes time to master.

KANJI

青 BLUE	台 BOARD	体 BODY	本 BOOK	借 BORROW	域 BOUNDED	明 BRIGHT	建 BUILD	
衣 CLOTHES	服 CLOTHING	雲 CLOUD	集 COLLECT	来 COME	委 COMMIT	社 COMPANY	写 COPY	
方 DIRECTION	医 DOCTOR	犬 DOG	下 DOWN	引 DRAW	画 DRAWING	飲 DRINK	早 EARLY	
夕 EVENING	毎 EVERY	高 EXPENSIVE	目 EYE	家 FAMILY	父 FATHER	羽 FEATHER	料 FEE	野 FIELD	火 FIRE	肉 FLESH	花 FLOWER	足 FOOT	友 FRIEND	从 FROM	示 GLORY
午 GO	金 GOLD	地 GROUND	半 HALF	堂 HALL	手 HAND	有 HAVE	聞 HEAR	心 HEART	天 HEAVENS	重 HEAVY	持 HOLD	屋 HOUSE	百 HUNDRED	病 ILLNESS	中 IN
院 INSTITUTION	間 INTERVAL	知 KNOW	語 LANGUAGE	学 LEARN	出 LEAVE	左 LEFT	貸 LEND	文 LETTER	生 LIFE	少 LITTLE	住 LIVE	愛 LOVE	主 MAIN	作 MAKE	男 MAN
営 MANAGE	多 MANY	印 MARK	飯 MEAL	員 MEMBER	意 MIND	分 MINUTE	口 MOUTH	山 MOUNTAIN	月 MOON	朝 MORNING	母 MOTHER	動 MOVE	名 NAME	新 NEW	夜 NIGHT
北 NORTH	不 NOT	洋 OCEAN	古 OLD	兄 OLDER BRO.	姉 OLDER SIS.	開 OPEN	元 ORIGIN	外 OUTSIDE	紙 PAPER	親 PARENT	通 PASS	色 PASSION	道 PATH	安 PEACEFUL	世 PERIOD
者 PERSON	場 PLACE	計 PLAN	楽 PLEASURE	位 POSITION	注 POUR	力 POWER	圧 PRESSURE	代 PRICE	私 PRIVATE	質 QUALITY	問 QUESTION	雨 RAIN	育 RAISE	読 READ	理 REASON
赤 RED	映 REFLECT	研 RESEARCH	休 REST	帰 RETURN	田 RICE FIELD	正 RIGHT	起 RISE	川 RIVER	室 ROOM	走 RUN	同 SAME	校 SCHOOL	海 SEA	見 SEE	自 SELF
売 SELL	送 SEND	話 SPEAK	別 SEPARATE	仕 SERVE	鋭 SHARP	店 SHOP	風 WIND	小 SMALL	会 SOCIETY	土 SOIL	歌 SONG	音 SOUND	南 SOUTH	言 SPEECH	気 SPIRIT
春 SPRING	立 STAND	発 START	駅 STATION	止 STOP	究 STUDY	服 SUBMIT	夏 SUMMER	日 SUN	英 SUPERB	泳 SWIM	味 TASTE	茶 TEA	万 TEN THOUSAND	験 TEST	物 THING
考 THINK	今 THIS	千 THOUSAND	時 TIME	題 TITLE	右 RIGHT	思 THINK	町 TOWN	旅 TRAVEL	木 TREE	真 TRUE	試 TRY	転 TURN	宇 UNIVERSE	上 UP	使 USE
車 VEHICLE	待 WAIT	歩 WALK	水 WATER	着 WEAR	週 WEEK	西 WEST	何 WHAT	白 WHITE	広 WIDE	冬 WINTER	界 WORLD	年 YEAR	円 YEN	弟 YOUNGER BRO.	妹 Y. SIS.

4 単語カード
tango kādo
vocabulary cards

3 漢字の学習は大切です。
Kanji no gakushū wa taisetsu desu.
Learning kanji characters is important.

5 書道
shodō
calligraphy

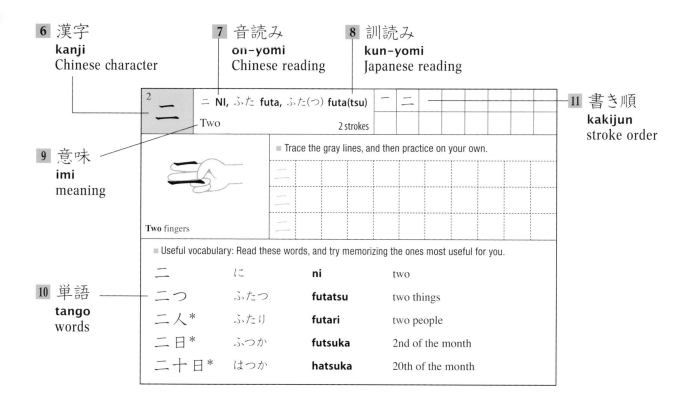

6 漢字
kanji
Chinese character

7 音読み
on-yomi
Chinese reading

8 訓読み
kun-yomi
Japanese reading

11 書き順
kakijun
stroke order

9 意味
imi
meaning

10 単語
tango
words

2 二	二 NI, ふた futa, ふた(つ) futa(tsu)	一 二
Two	2 strokes	

Two fingers

■ Trace the gray lines, and then practice on your own.

■ Useful vocabulary: Read these words, and try memorizing the ones most useful for you.

二	に	**ni**	two
二つ	ふたつ	**futatsu**	two things
二人*	ふたり	**futari**	two people
二日*	ふつか	**futsuka**	2nd of the month
二十日*	はつか	**hatsuka**	20th of the month

Additional Vocabulary

12 日本語
Nihongo
Japanese language

13 語彙
goi
vocabulary

14 アクセント
akusento
accent

15 熟語
jukugo
idiom

16 文章
bunshō
sentence

17 文句
monku
phrase

18 作文
sakubun
short essay

19 詩
shi; uta
poem

20 論文
ronbun
thesis; dissertation

21 文化
bunka
culture

22 文法
bunpō
grammar

23 翻訳
hon'yaku
translation

24 語学
gogaku
linguistics

25 レッスン
ressun
lesson

26 コース
kōsu
course; academic program

27 宿題
shukudai
assignment

28 練習帳
renshūchō
exercise book

29 簡単
kantan
simple

30 理解する
rikai suru
to understand

31 易しい
yasashii
easy

32 難しい
muzukashii
difficult

33 訓練する
kunren suru
to drill

34 一生懸命
isshōkenmei
to strive

35 準備する
junbi suru
to prepare

22 助数詞
Josūshi
Counting Words
Also known as "measure words"

2 一人、二人、三人…
hitori, futari, sannin …
people counter

1 一つ、二つ、三つ…
hitotsu, futatsu, mittsu …
general object counter

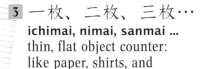

3 一枚、二枚、三枚…
ichimai, nimai, sanmai …
thin, flat object counter: like paper, shirts, and tickets

4 一本、二本、三本…
ippon, nihon, sanbon …
long, cylindrical object counter: like pencils, flowers, and trees

5 一台、二台、三台…
ichidai, nidai, sandai …
machines: like cars and computers

6 一杯、二杯、三杯…
ippai, nipai, sanpai …
cups and glasses of drink; spoonful

7 一匹、二匹、三匹…
ippiki, nihiki, sanbiki …
small animals

8 一頭、二頭、三頭…
ittō, nitō, santō …
large animals

9 一個、二個、三個…
ikko, niko, sanko …
small or round objects

10 一冊、二冊、三冊…
issatsu, nisatsu, sansatsu …
books, notes

Counting words or measure words are used to quantify things, just as in English we say "three sheets of paper" or "two cups of coffee." Some common measure words in Japanese are listed below.

11	階 kai/gai	floors of a building	あのビルの一階にあります。 **Ano biru no ikkai ni arimasu.** It's on the first floor of that building.
12	度 do	occurrences, times, degrees	もう一度言ってください。 **Mō ichido itte kudasai.** Please repeat that.
13	回 kai	occurrences, times	彼は週に三回塾に行く。 **Kare wa shū ni sankai juku ni iku.** He attends cram school three times per week.
14	キロ kiro	kilometers, kilograms	その会社の人は一ヶ月に三万五千キロ飛行機で移動します。 **Sono kaisha no hito wa ikkagetsu ni sanman gosen kiro hikōki de idō shimasu.** That company's employees fly 35,000 kilometers per month.
15	マイル mairu	miles	郵便局は半マイル向こうにある。 **Yūbinkyoku wa hanmairu mukō ni aru.** The post office is half a mile that way.
16	名 mei	people (honorific)	何名様ですか。 **Nanmei-sama desu ka.** How many people (honorific)?
17	秒 byō	seconds	私は30秒で電車に乗り遅れました。 **Watashi wa sanjūbyō de densha ni noriokure-mashita.** I missed my train by 30 seconds.
18	分 fun; pun	minutes	学校まで10分で歩いて行ける。 **Gakkō made juppun de aruite ikeru.** I can walk to school in ten minutes.
19	時 ji	hours of the day	もう11時ですよ。 **Mō jūichiji desu yo.** It's already 11 o'clock.
20	時間 jikan	hours	あの店は24時間開いている。 **Ano mise wa nijūyojikan aite iru.** That store is open 24 hours.
21	泊 haku; paku	night stays	料金は、税別で一泊100ドルです。 **Ryōkin wa, zeibetsu de ippaku hyakudoru desu.** The fee is 100 dollars per night, plus tax.
22	ヶ月 kagetsu	months	彼女は妊娠八ヶ月です。 **Kanojo wa ninshin hachikagetsu desu.** She is eight months pregnant.
23	年 nen	years	私は三年前に日本に来ました。 **Watashi wa sannen mae ni Nihon ni kimashita.** I came to Japan three years ago.

23 コンピューターと インターネット

Konpyūtā to intānetto

Computers and the Internet

2 画面
gamen
screen

1 コンピューター
konpyūtā
computers

3 タブレット
taburetto
tablet

6 ラップトップ
rapputoppu
laptop

4 デスクトップ・
コンピューター
desukutoppu konpyūtā
desktop computer

5 キーボード
kiibōdo
keyboard

7 日本では、インターネットを使う
のが簡単です。
**Nihon dewa, intānetto o tsukau
no ga kantan desu.**
It's easy to use the internet in Japan.

10 マウス
mausu
mouse

8 テレビゲーム
terebi gēmu
video game

9 マウスパッド
mausupaddo
mousepad

11 スキャンする
sukyan suru
to scan

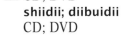

12 CD; DVD
shiidii; diibuidii
CD; DVD

13 ユーエスビーフラ
ッシュドライブ
**yūesubii furasshu
doraibu**
USB flash drive

14 ポート
pōto
ports

15 電子メール**denshi
mēru**
email

16 ログイン
roguin
to sign in

17 パスワード
pasuwādo
password

18 ウェブサイト
webusaito
website

19 ソフト（ウェア）
sofuto (wea)
software

20 オペレーティングシステム; OS
operētingu shisutemu; ōesu
operating system

21 ウィルス
wirusu
virus

22 ファイル
fairu
file

23 ネットワーク
nettowāku
network

24 ウェブページ
webu pēji
web page

25 ウェブデザイン
webu dezain
web design

26 ウェブアドレス
webuadoresu
web address; URL

27 アプリケーション
apurikēshon
application (computer program)

28 インターネットアクセス
intānetto akusesu
Internet access

29 クリックする
kurikku suru
to click

30 ダウンロードする
daunrōdo suru
to download

31 インターネットを使う
intānetto o tsukau
to use the internet

32 オンライン
onrain
online

33 チャットルーム
chatto rūmu
chat room

34 ネットワークカード
nettowāku kādo
network card

35 マルチメディア
maruchimedia
multimedia

36 ブログ
burogu
blog

37 ブラウザ
burauza
browser

38 チャットする
chatto suru
to chat online

39 ネットワークセキュリティー
nettowāku sekyuritii
network security

40 電子メールを送る
denshi mēru o okuru
to send an email

41 検索する
kensaku suru
to search online

42 WiFi
waifai
wifi

43 ケーブルネットワーク
kēburu nettowāku
cable network

44 によって
ni yotte
according to

45 後で
ato de
after that

46 だから; なので
dakara; nanode
because

47 しかも
shikamo
in addition

48 非常に
hijō ni
very; extremely

50 一緒にチャットしませんか。
Issho ni chatto shimasen ka.
Let's chat online.

51 どのアプリを使いますか。
私はラインを使います。
Dono apuri o tsukaimasu ka. Watashi wa rain o tsukaimasu.
What app do you use? I use LINE.

52 はい、今書類をメールでそちらへ送ります。
Hai, ima shorui o mēru de sochira e okurimasu.
Okay, I'm now sending you the documents via computer.

49 僕の趣味はオンラインゲームをすることです。
Boku no shumi wa onrain gēmu o suru koto desu.
My hobby is online gaming.

私のスマホ

Watashi no sumaho
24 | My Smartphone

1 スマホ; スマートフォン
sumaho; sumātofon
smartphone

2 ネット友達
netto tomodachi
online friends

3 オンライン
ショッピング
onrain shoppingu
online shopping

4 ネットカフェ
netto kafe
internet cafes

5 ツイッター
Tsuittā
Twitter

6 ライン
Rain
LINE

7 アンドロイド 携帯
Andoroido keitai
Android phones

8 アイフォン
aifon
iPhones

9 携帯電話
keitai denwa
mobile phone

10 電話をかける
denwa o kakeru
to make a phone call

11 電話を受ける
denwa o ukeru
to receive a phone call

Additional Vocabulary

24 電話番号
denwa bangō
telephone number

25 ネットワーク;
インターネット
nettowāku; intānetto
network; Internet

26 インターネット言語
intānetto gengo
Internet language

27 ショートメッセージ
shōto messēji
texting

28 インターネットスラング
intānetto surangu
Internet slang

29 充電器
jūdenki
phone charger

30 テレホンカード
terehon kādo
phone cards

31 市外電話
shigai denwa
long distance call

32 国番号
kuni bangō
country code

33 市外局番
shigai kyokuban
area code

34 動画
dōga
video

35 SIMカード
shimu kādo
SIM card

14 セルフィー；
自撮り
serufii; jidori
selfie

12 電波が強い
denpa ga tsuyoi
strong signal

13 電波が弱い
（悪い）
**denpa ga yowai
(warui)**
weak signal

15 グルーフィー
gurūfii
wefie; groufie

Some common telephone phrases:

36 もしもし／（名前）です。
Moshi moshi/(namae) desu.
Hello? / This is (name).

37 すみませんが、（名前）さん
いらっしゃいますか。
Sumimasen ga, (namae) san irasshaimasu ka.
May I speak to (name)?

38 折り返しお電話をお願いします。
Orikaeshi odenwa o onegai shimasu.
Please ask him/her to return my call.

39 今お電話いいでしょうか。
Ima odenwa ii deshō ka.
Is it convenient to talk now?

40 大きい声で話してください。
Ōkii koe de hanashite kudasai.
Could you speak up?

41 間違い電話です。
Machigai denwa desu.
Sorry, you dialed the wrong number.

42 少々お待ちください。
Shōshō omachi kudasai.
Please wait a moment.

43 伝言を残してください。
Dengon o nokoshite kudasai.
Please leave a message.

44 どちら様でしょうか。
Dochira-sama deshō ka.
Who's calling, please?

45 ゆっくり話してください。
Yukkuri hanashite kudasai.
Could you speak a little slower?

16 ソニー
Sonii
Sony

17 任天堂
Nintendō
Nintendo

18 フェイスブック
Feisubukku
Facebook

19 グーグル
Gūguru
Google

20 ニコン
Nikon
Nikon

21 ホンダ
Honda
Honda

22 アップル
Appuru
Apple

23 マイクロソフト
Maikurosofuto
Microsoft

25

職場で
Shokuba de
At Work

1 弁護士
bengoshi
lawyer

2 裁判官
saibankan
judge

9 建築家
kenchikuka
architect

10 オペレーター
operētā
telephone operator

3 投資家
tōshika
financier

4 エンジニア
enjinia
engineer

15 事務所; オフィス
jimusho; ofisu
office

5 会計士
kaikeishi
accountant

6 薬剤師
yakuzaishi
pharmacist

7 芸術家
geijutsuka
artist

8 音楽家
ongakuka
musician

16 管理職
kanrishoku
manager

17 秘書
hisho
secretary

11 シェフ; コック
shefu; kokku
chef

12 写真家
shashinka
photographer

13 パイロット
pairotto
pilot

14 歯医者
haisha
dentist

18 消防士
shōbōshi
firefighter

19 農家
nōka
farmer

Additional Vocabulary

20 会社
kaisha
company

21 企業家
kigyōka
entrepreneur

22 調べる
shiraberu
to inspect

23 出勤する
shukkin suru
to go to work

24 同僚
dōryō
colleague

25 仕事
shigoto
work

26 職員; 社員
shokuin; shain
staff; personnel;
employee

27 見習い
minarai
apprentice

28 インターン
intān
intern

29 アルバイト
arubaito
part-time job

30 残業する
zangyō suru
to work
overtime

31 ウェイター;
ウェイトレス
**weitā;
weitoresu**
waiter;
waitress

32 方法
hōhō
method

33 機会
kikai
opportunity

34 職
shoku
position

35 いつも
itsumo
always

36 仕事は何をしていますか。私は病院で働いています。
Shigoto wa nani o shite imasu ka. Watashi wa byōin de hataraite imasu.
What sort of work do you do? I work in a hospital.

37 私は研修医をしています。
Watashi wa kenshūi o shite imasu.
I'm training to be a doctor.

38 私は毎朝8時45分に出勤します。
Watashi wa hachiji yonjūgofun ni shukkin shimasu.
I go to work at 8:45 a.m. every morning.

音楽と踊り

26

Ongaku to odori

Music and Dance

1 ギター
gitā
guitar

2 琴
koto
long zither with 13 strings

4 バイオリン
baiorin
violin

3 三味線
shamisen
a banjo-like lute with three strings

5 尺八
shakuhachi
a vertical bamboo flute

6 踊る; ダンスする
odoru; dansu suru
to dance

7 ドラム
doramu
drums

8 トランペット
toranpetto
trumpet

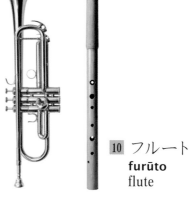

9 ピアノ
piano
piano

10 フルート
furūto
flute

11 カラオケ
karaoke
karaoke

12 歌を歌う
uta o utau
to sing

13 コンサート
konsāto
concert

14 観客
kankyaku
audience

15 ポップグループ
poppu gurūpu
pop group

16 歌舞伎
Kabuki
Kabuki
theater

17 俳優; 女優
haiyū; joyū
actor; actress

19 楽しむ
tanoshimu
to appreciate;
to enjoy

20 音楽
ongaku
music

21 舞踊
buyō
dance
(performance art)

22 上演する
jōen suru
to perform

23 演目
enmoku
program

24 ポップス
poppusu
pop music

25 弾く
hiku
to play a string
instrument

26 イヤホン
iyahon
earphones

27 演奏する
ensō suru
to perform
(on a musical
instrument)

28 楽団
gakudan
band; orchestra

29 歌手
kashu
singer

30 趣味
shumi
hobby

31 有名
yūmei
famous

32 表現する
hyōgen suru
to express

18 チェロ
chero
cello

33 ギターを弾くことができますか。
Gitā o hiku koto ga dekimasu ka.
Can you play the guitar?

34 どんな音楽が好きですか。
Donna ongaku ga suki desu ka.
What kind of music do you like?

医者に診てもらう

Isha ni mite morau

27 Seeing a Doctor

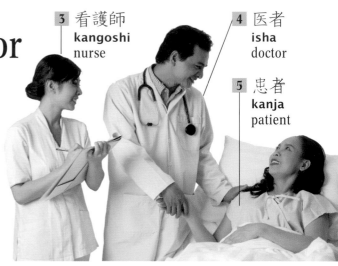

3 看護師
kangoshi
nurse

4 医者
isha
doctor

5 患者
kanja
patient

1 病院
byōin
hospital

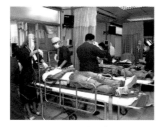

2 救急救命室
kyūkyū-kyūmeishitsu
emergency room

6 採血
saiketsu
to draw blood

7 血液検査
ketsueki kensa
blood test

8 実験
jikken
laboratory test

9 血圧
ketsuatsu
blood pressure

10 風邪をひく
kaze o hiku
to catch a cold

11 咳が出る
seki ga deru
to cough

12 熱
netsu
fever

13 病気になる
byōki ni naru
to fall sick

14 薬を飲む
kusuri o nomu
to take
medicine

15 薬
kusuri
medicine

16 錠剤
jōzai
pills

17 注射
chūsha
injection

18 診察室
shinsatsushitsu
doctor's consultation
room

19 待合室
machiaishitsu
waiting room

20 予約
yoyaku
appointment

21 救急車
kyūkyūsha
ambulance

22 歯科
shika
dentistry

23 内科
naika
general medicine

24 外科
geka
general surgery

25 耳鼻科
jibika
ear, nose, and
throat

26 小児科
shōnika
pediatrics

27 産婦人科
sanfujinka
gynecology

28 眼科
ganka
ophthalmology

29 皮膚科
hifuka
dermatology

30 腫瘍科
shuyōka
oncology

31 理学療法
rigaku ryōhō
physiotherapy

32 神経内科
shinkeinaika
neurology

33 放射線科
hōshasenka
radiology

34 事故
jiko
accident

35 処方箋
shohōsen
prescription

36 消毒剤
shōdokuzai
antiseptic

37 軟膏
nankō
ointment

38 傷口
kizuguchi
wound; cut

39 救急
kyūkyū
emergency

40 痛い
itai
hurts

41 疲れている
tsukarete iru
tired; worn out

42 感じがする
kanji ga suru
to feel

43 何度か
nando ka
several times

44 心配
shinpai
anxious; worried

45 見つける
mitsukeru
to discover

46 安心する
anshin suru
to feel reassured

47 心配する
shinpai suru
to be concerned
about

48 … に関する
… ni kansuru
pertaining to

49 希望
kibō
hope

50 重要な
jūyō na
important

51 主な
omo na
main

52 救急箱
kyūkyū-bako
first aid kit

53 包帯
hōtai
bandage

54 どうしましたか。
Dō shimashita ka.
What is wrong?

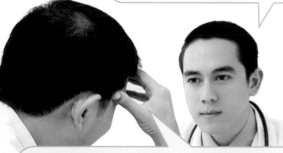

55 熱があります。そして喉が痛いです。
Netsu ga arimasu. Soshite nodo ga itai desu.
I have a fever and a sore throat.

56 具合が悪いです。
Guai ga warui desu.
I am not feeling well.

57 医者に診てもらいたいです。
Isha ni mite moraitai desu.
I would like to see a doctor.

58 予約していますか。
Yoyaku shite imasu ka.
Do you have an appointment?

28 環境を守る
Kankyō o mamoru
Protecting Our Environment

1 庭園; 庭
teien; niwa
garden

2 花
hana
flower

6 電気自動車
denki jidōsha
electric car

3 公園
kōen
park

4 公害
kōgai
pollution

5 草
kusa
grass

7 海
umi
ocean

8 川
kawa
river

9 太陽エネルギー
taiyō enerugii
solar energy

10 静か
shizuka
quiet

40 ここの空気はきれいです。
Koko no kūki wa kirei desu.
The air here is really fresh!

12 風力
fūryoku
wind power

11 空気
kūki
air

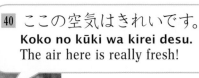

13 森
mori
forest

14 林
hayashi
grove

15 木
ki
tree

16 天然ガス
tennen-gasu
natural gas

17 原子力
genshiryoku
nuclear energy

18 きれい
kirei
clean

19 植える
ueru
plant

20 リサイクル
risaikuru
recycling

21 クリーン
エネルギー
kuriin enerugii
clean energy

22 石油
sekiyu
oil

23 石炭
sekitan
coal

24 空気の質
kūki no shitsu
air quality

25 指標
shihyō
index

26 水
mizu
water

27 清潔
seiketsu
clean

28 環境
kankyō
environment

29 マスク
masuku
mask

30 変化
henka
changes

31 地面; 大地
jimen; daichi
earth; ground

32 … のために
... no tame ni
for the purpose of

33 できる
dekiru
can; to be able to

34 完成する
kansei suru
to accomplish

35 影響する
eikyō suru
to affect

36 でも; しかし
demo; shikashi
but; however

37 もちろん
mochiron
of course

38 のに
no ni
although

39 から
kara
as a result of

41 リサイクルしますか。
Risaikuru shimasu ka.
Do you recycle?

42 私はガラスと紙、プラスチック
をリサイクルします。
**Watashi wa garasu to kami,
purasuchikku o risaikuru shimasu.**
I recycle glass, paper and plastic.

65

動物界

Dōbutsukai

29 The Animal Kingdom

3 キリン
kirin
giraffe

1 動物園
dōbutsuen
zoo

2 シマウマ
shimauma
zebra

4 トラ
tora
tiger

5 ライオン
raion
lion

> **29** この動物の方がその動物より小さいです。
> **Kono dōbutsu no hō ga sono dōbutsu yori chiisai desu.**
> This animal is smaller than that one.
>
> **30** 動物園に行くのが好きですか。
> **Dōbutsuen ni iku no ga suki desu ka.**
> Do you like going to the zoo?
>
> **31** 動物園には、動物がたくさんいます。
> **Dōbutsuen ni wa, dōbutsu ga takusan imasu.**
> There are many animals in the zoo.

6 熊
kuma
bear

10 恐竜
kyōryū
dinosaur

7 猿
saru
monkey

8 ゴリラ
gorira
gorilla

9 パンダ
panda
panda

11 ヤギ
yagi
goat

12 羊
hitsuji
sheep

13 牛
ushi
cow

32 すごい
sugoi
great; wonderful; terrible

33 怖い
kowai
afraid

14 象
zō
elephant

15 馬
uma
horse

16 オオカミ
ōkami
wolf

34 可愛い
kawaii
cute; adorable

35 それ
sore
that

36 とても
totemo
very; extremely

17 蛇
hebi
snake

18 孔雀
kujaku
peacock

19 鶏
niwatori
chicken

20 鳥
tori
bird

37 似ている
nite iru
similar; alike

38 に見える
ni mieru
to look like; to resemble

39 現れる
arawareru
to appear

21 犬
inu
dog

22 猫
neko
cat

23 竜; 龍
tatsu; ryū
dragon

40 敢えて
aete
to dare

41 不思議
fushigi
strange

24 蚊
ka
mosquito

25 ハエ
hae
housefly

26 蜂; 蜜蜂
hachi; mitsubachi
bee; honeybee

27 蝶
chō
butterfly

28 魚
sakana
fish

健康を保とう！

Kenkō o tamotō

30 | Let's Keep Fit!

1 卓球
takkyū
table tennis

2 サッカー
sakkā
soccer

3 ラグビー
ragubii
rugby

4 山登り
yamanobori
mountain climbing

5 バドミントン
badominton
badminton

6 運動する
undō suru
to exercise; sports

7 野球
yakyū
baseball

9 ランニング
ranningu
running

10 長距離走
chōkyorisō
long-distance running

11 自転車
jitensha
bicycle

8 短距離走
tankyorisō
sprint

12 自転車に乗る
jitensha ni noru
to cycle

13 競技会；試合
kyōgikai; shiai
competition; game

14 ゴール
gōru
finish line

15 ゴルフ
gorufu
golf

16 アイススケート
aisu sukēto
ice-skating

17 スキー
sukii
skiing

18 ボート競技
bōto kyōgi
rowing

19 水泳
suiei
swimming

Additional Vocabulary

25 トレーナー
torēnā
sports shirt;
sweatshirt

26 スニーカー
suniikā
sports shoes;
sneakers

27 ボール
bōru
ball

28 健康
kenkō
healthy

20 バレーボール
barēbōru
volleyball

21 歩く
aruku
walking

22 テニス
tenisu
tennis

23 ラケット
raketto
racket

29 運動するのが好きですか。
Undō suru no ga suki desu ka.
Do you like to exercise?

30 どんなスポーツをしますか。
Donna supōtsu o shimasu ka.
What sports do you play?

31 私はジョギングと野球が好きです。
**Watashi wa jogingu to yakyū ga
suki desu.**
I like to jog and play basketball.

24 バスケットボール
basukettobōru
basketball

69

旅行が好き？

Ryokō ga suki?

31 | Do You Like to Travel?

3 旅行者
ryokōsha
traveler

4 荷物
nimotsu
luggage

5 スーツケース
sūtsukēsu
suitcase

1 ホテル
hoteru
hotel

2 地図
chizu
map

6 ガイド
gaido
tour guide

7 観光地
kankōchi
tourist attraction

8 パスポート
pasupōto
passport

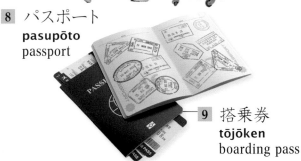

9 搭乗券
tōjōken
boarding pass

10 飛行機で旅行する
hikōki de ryokō suru
travel by airplane

11 電車で旅行する
densha de ryokō suru
travel by rail

12 観光バスで旅行する
kankōbasu de ryokō suru
travel by bus

13 客船
kyakusen
cruise ship

14 土産物店
miyagemonoten
souvenir shop

15 カメラ
kamera
camera

16 写真
shashin
photograph

17 旅行
ryokō
a trip; to travel

18 休み
yasumi
vacation

19 航空券
kōkūken
plane ticket

20 ホテルの予約
hoteru no yoyaku
hotel reservation

21 通貨
tsūka
currency

22 ビザ
biza
visa

23 旅行ガイドブック
ryokō gaidobukku
travel guidebook

24 旅行会社
ryokō gaisha
travel agency

25 予防接種
yobō sesshu
vaccination

26 ユースホステル
yūsu hosuteru
youth hostel

27 税関
zeikan
customs

28 観光
kankō
sightseeing

29 観光案内所
kankō annaisho
tourist information center

30 葉書
hagaki
postcard

31 無料Wi-Fi
muryō waifai
free wifi

32 博物館
hakubutsukan
museum

33 海; 浜
umi; hama
beach

34 記念碑
kinenhi
monument

35 駅
eki
train station

36 空港
kūkō
airport

37 客船案内所
kyakusen annaisho
cruise center

38 民宿
minshuku
guesthouse; lodge

39 レストラン
resutoran
restaurant

40 探す; 見つける
sagasu; mitsukeru
to find

41 取る
toru
to take

42 出会う
deau
to come across

43 注意する
chūi suru
to pay attention to

44 気づく
kizuku
to become aware of

45 他
hoka
another; other

46 他人
tanin
others

47 かもしれない
kamoshirenai
maybe

48 どこへ旅行するのが好きですか。
Doko e ryokō suru no ga suki desu ka.
Where do you like to go on vacation?

49 私は東京が好きです。
Watashi wa Tōkyō ga suki desu.
I like to vacation in Tokyo.

50 大阪への指定席券をお願いします。
Ōsaka e no shiteisekiken o onegai shimasu.
I'd like a reserved train ticket to Osaka.

51 彼は世界一周の旅をしました。
Kare wa sekai isshū no tabi o shimashita.
He made a round-the-world trip.

52 マイレージを貯めるために、いつも同じ航空会社を使っています。
Mairēji o tameru tame ni, itsumo onaji kōkū–gaisha o tsukatte imasu.
I always use the same airlines to get mileage points.

世界の国々

Sekai no kuni guni

32 | Countries of the World

1 東南アジア諸国
Tōnan Ajia shokoku
Countries in Southeast Asia

2 タイ
Tai
Thailand

3 ミャンマー
Myanmā
Myanmar

4 ベトナム
Betonamu
Vietnam

5 フィリピン
Firipin
Philippines

6 ラオス
Raosu
Laos

7 カンボジア
Kanbojia
Cambodia

8 マレーシア
Marēshia
Malaysia

9 ブルネイ
Burunei
Brunei

10 シンガポール
Shingapōru
Singapore

11 インドネシア
Indoneshia
Indonesia

12 東ティモール
Higashi Timōru
East Timor

---

30 私たちは日本で結婚式をするつもりです。
Watashitachi wa Nihon de kekkonshiki o suru tsumori desu.
We intend to hold our wedding ceremony in Japan.

31 どこの国から来ましたか。私はアメリカ人です。
Doko no kuni kara kimashita ka. Watashi wa Amerikajin desu.
What country are you from? I am American.

13 世界の七大陸
Sekai no nanatairiku
Seven continents of the world

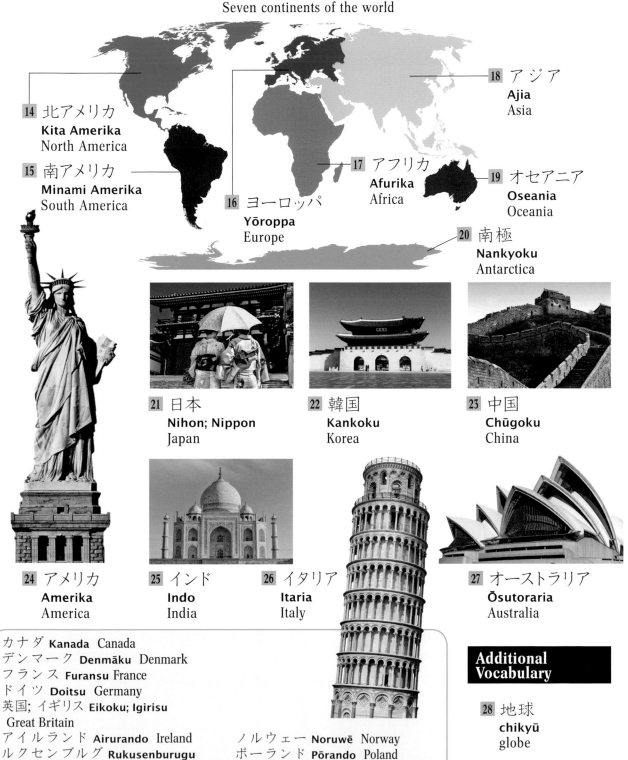

14 北アメリカ
Kita Amerika
North America

15 南アメリカ
Minami Amerika
South America

16 ヨーロッパ
Yōroppa
Europe

17 アフリカ
Afurika
Africa

18 アジア
Ajia
Asia

19 オセアニア
Oseania
Oceania

20 南極
Nankyoku
Antarctica

21 日本
Nihon; Nippon
Japan

22 韓国
Kankoku
Korea

23 中国
Chūgoku
China

24 アメリカ
Amerika
America

25 インド
Indo
India

26 イタリア
Itaria
Italy

27 オーストラリア
Ōsutoraria
Australia

カナダ **Kanada** Canada
デンマーク **Denmāku** Denmark
フランス **Furansu** France
ドイツ **Doitsu** Germany
英国; イギリス **Eikoku; Igirisu**
 Great Britain
アイルランド **Airurando** Ireland
ルクセンブルグ **Rukusenburugu**
 Luxembourg
オランダ **Oranda** Netherlands
ニュージーランド **Nyūjiirando**
 New Zealand

ノルウェー **Noruwē** Norway
ポーランド **Pōrando** Poland
ロシア **Roshia** Russia
スウェーデン **Suwēden** Sweden
スイス **Suisu** Switzerland
バチカン **Bachikan** Vatican

Additional Vocabulary

28 地球
chikyū
globe

29 世界
sekai
world

外国語
Gaikokugo

33 Foreign Languages

Hello!

1 英語
Eigo
English

Bonjour!

2 フランス語
Furansugo
French

привет

3 ロシア語
Roshiago
Russian

Guten Tag!

4 ドイツ語
Doltsugo
German

Ciao!

5 イタリア語
Itariago
Italian

¡Hola!

6 スペイン語
Supeingo
Spanish

Merhaba!

7 トルコ語
Torukogo
Turkish

こんにちは

8 日本語
Nihongo
Japanese

مرحبا

9 アラビア語
Arabiago
Arabic

Χαίρετε

שלום

Xin chào!

10 ギリシャ語
Girishago
Greek

11 ヘブライ語
Heburaigo
Hebrew

12 ベトナム語
Betonamugo
Vietnamese

สวัสดี

नमस्ते

Apa kabar

13 ヒンディー語
Hindiigo
Hindi

14 インドネシア語
Indoneshiago
Indonesian

15 タイ語
Taigo
Thai

안녕하세요

Olá!

你好！

Kamusta

17 タガログ語
Tagarogugo
Tagalog

18 ポルトガル語
Porutogarugo
Portuguese

19 中国語
Chūgokugo
Chinese

16 韓国語
Kankokugo
Korean

---

20 母国語は何ですか。
Bokokugo wa nan desu ka.
What is your mother tongue?

21 何ヶ国語が話せますか。
Nankakokugo ga hanasemasu ka.
How many languages do you speak?

和食は好き？
Washoku wa suki?
34 | Do You Like Japanese Food?

1 定食
teishoku
set menu

2 ウェイター；
ウェイトレス
weitā; weitoresu
waiter; waitress

3 シェフ；コック
shefu; kokku
chef; cook

4 メニュー
menyū
menu

5 ご飯
gohan
cooked rice

6 チャーハン
chāhan
fried rice

7 パン
pan
bread

8 箸
hashi
chopsticks

12 フォーク
fōku
fork

13 ナイフ
naifu
knife

9 茶碗
chawan
bowl

11 皿
sara
plate

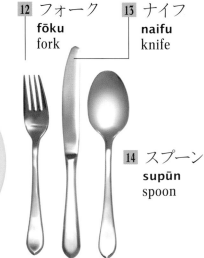

14 スプーン
supūn
spoon

10 白いご飯
shiroi gohan
white rice

15 餃子
gyōza
fried dumplings

16 うどん
udon
thick wheat noodles

17 そば
soba
buckwheat noodles

18 ラーメン
rāmen
ramen noodles

19 刺身
sashimi
sliced raw fish

20 寿司
sushi
sushi

21 天ぷら
tenpura
tempura

Additional Vocabulary

25 スープ
sūpu
soup

26 菜食
saishoku
vegetarian

27 注文する
chūmon suru
to order

28 選択
sentaku
choice

29 特別
tokubetsu
special

30 それに
sore ni
also; too

22 焼肉
yakiniku
roasted beef with dipping sauce

23 焼き鳥
yakitori
roasted chicken kebab

24 たこ焼き
takoyaki
ball-shaped snack with octopus

31 それとも
soretomo
or (commonly used between sentences)

32 だいたい
daitai
almost

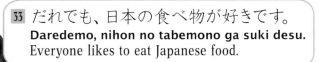

33 だれでも、日本の食べ物が好きです。
Daredemo, nihon no tabemono ga suki desu.
Everyone likes to eat Japanese food.

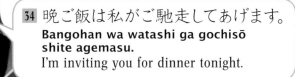

34 晩ご飯は私がご馳走してあげます。
Bangohan wa watashi ga gochisō shite agemasu.
I'm inviting you for dinner tonight.

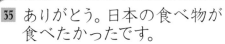

35 ありがとう。日本の食べ物が食べたかったです。
Arigatō. Nihon no tabemono ga tabetakatta desu.
That's great! I want to eat Japanese food.

36 すみません
Sumimasen
Excuse me ... (call a waiter/waitress)

人気の洋食
Ninki no yōshoku
Popular Western Foods

1 ホットドッグ
hotto doggu
hot dog

2 サンドイッチ
sandoitchi
sandwich

3 ピザ
piza
pizza

4 パスタ;
スパゲッティ
pasuta; supagetti
pasta; spaghetti

5 ドーナッツ
dōnattsu
donuts

6 フランスパン
furansupan
baguette

7 アイスクリーム
aisu kuriimu
ice cream

8 プリン
purin
pudding

9 ラザニア
razania
lasagne

10 七面鳥
shichimenchō
turkey

11 アップルパイ
appuru pai
apple pie

12 ハム
hamu
ham

13 サラダ
sarada
salad

15 ステーキ
sutēki
steak

14 マッシュ
ポテト
masshu poteto
mashed potatoes

16 ソーセージ
sōsēji
sausage

17 洋風の朝食
Yōfū no chōshoku
Western breakfast

18 ジュース
jūsu
juice

19 コーヒー
kōhii
coffee

20 ベーコン
bēkon
bacon

21 卵焼き; 目玉焼き
tamagoyaki; medamayaki
sunny side up eggs

22 トースト
tōsuto
toast

日本の人気ファストフード店
Nihon no ninki fasutofūdo-ten
Some popular fast food chains in Japan

スターバックス
Sutābakkusu
Starbucks

マクドナルド
Makudonarudo
McDonald's

ケンタッキー
フライドチキン
**Kentakkii
furaido chikin**
Kentucky Fried
Chicken

ピザハット
Pizahatto
Pizza Hut

サブウェイ
Sabuwei
Subway

ハーゲンダッツ
Hāgendattsu
Haagen-Dazs

23 ケーキ
kēki
cake

24 チーズ
chiizu
cheese

25 シリアル
shiriaru
cereal

26 オートミール
ōtomiiru
oatmeal; rolled oats

Additional Vocabulary

29 洋食
Yōshoku
Western-style food

30 美味しい
oishii
tasty; delicious

31 バーベキュー
bābekyū
barbecue

32 焼く
yaku
to roast; to bake

33 ホットケーキ
hotto kēki
pancakes

34 バター; クリーム
batā; kuriimu
butter; cream

35 ヨーグルト
yōguruto
yogurt

36 ケチャップ
kechappu
ketchup;
tomato sauce

37 日本ではマクドナルドはとても人気があります。
Nihon dewa Makudonarudo wa totemo ninki ga arimasu.
McDonald's is a popular fast food restaurant in Japan.

38 若者の多くはハンバーガーやポテトフライが好きです。
Wakamono no ōku wa hanbāgā ya potetofurai ga suki desu.
All children like hamburgers and french fries.

39 和食と洋食ではどちらの方が好きですか。
Washoku to yōshoku dewa, dochira no hō ga suki desu ka.
Do you prefer Japanese food or Western food?

27 ハンバーガー
hanbāgā
hamburger

28 ポテト
フライ
**poteto-
furai**
french
fries

37

Fresh Fruits, Nuts and Grains

1 りんご
ringo
apple

2 マンゴー
mangō
mango

3 オレンジ
orenji
orange

4 みかん
mikan
mandarin orange

5 なし
nashi
pear

6 ココナッツ
kokonattsu
coconut

7 バナナ
banana
banana

8 パイナップル
painappuru
pineapple

9 桃
momo
peach

10 パパイヤ
papaiya
papaya

11 レモン
remon
lemon

12 ライム
raimu
lime

13 ライチ
raichi
lychee

14 リュウガン
ryūgan
longan

15 いちご
ichigo
strawberry

16 ぶどう
budō
grapes

17 マスクメロン
masukumeron
cantaloupe

18 柿
kaki
persimmon

19 スイカ
suika
watermelon

49 私は新鮮な果物を食べるのが好きです。
Watashi wa shinsen na furūtsu o taberu no ga suki desu.
I love to eat fresh fruits.

20 ピーナッツ
piinattsu
peanuts

21 くるみ
kurumi
walnuts

22 ピーカン
ナッツ
piikan nattsu
pecans

23 ピスタチオ
pisutachio
pistachios

24 アーモンド
āmondo
almonds

29 カシューナッツ
kashū nattsu
cashew nuts

25 マカデミアナッツ
makademia nattsu
macadamia nuts

26 栗
kuri
chestnuts

27 ヘーゼル
ナッツ
hēzeru nattsu
hazel nuts

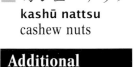

28 松の実
matsu no mi
pine nuts

Additional Vocabulary

40 穀物
kokumotsu
grains; cereals

41 ナッツ
nattsu
nuts

42 クラッカー
kurakkā
crackers

43 オートミール
ōtomiiru
oatmeal

44 ドライ
フルーツ
dorai furūtsu
dried fruits

45 豆
mame
beans

46 とうもろこし
tōmorokoshi
corn

47 小麦粉
komugiko
flour

48 アレルギー
arerugii
to be allergic;
allergy

30 カボチャの種
kabocha no tane
pumpkin seeds

31 スイカの種
suika no tane
watermelon
seeds

32 ヒマワリの種
himawari no tane
sunflower seeds

33 ゴマ
goma
sesame seeds

34 オーツ麦
ōtsu mugi
oats

35 大麦
ōmugi
barley

36 キビ
kibi
millet

37 そば
soba
buckwheat

38 米
kome
rice

39 小麦
komugi
wheat

51 どんなナッツが好きですか。
Donna nattsu ga suki desu ka.
What nuts do you like?

52 私は松の実が好きです。
あなたはどうですか？
Watashi wa matsu no mi ga suki desu.
Anata wa dō desu ka?
I like pine nuts. What about you?

53 私はナッツのアレルギーが
あります。
Watashi wa nattsu no arerugii ga
arimasu.
I am allergic to nuts.

50 ナッツなしのサラダの
おかわりをください。
Nattsu nashi no sarada no
okawari o kudasai.
Can I have one more salad
without nuts?

38

スーパーで
Sūpā de
At the Market

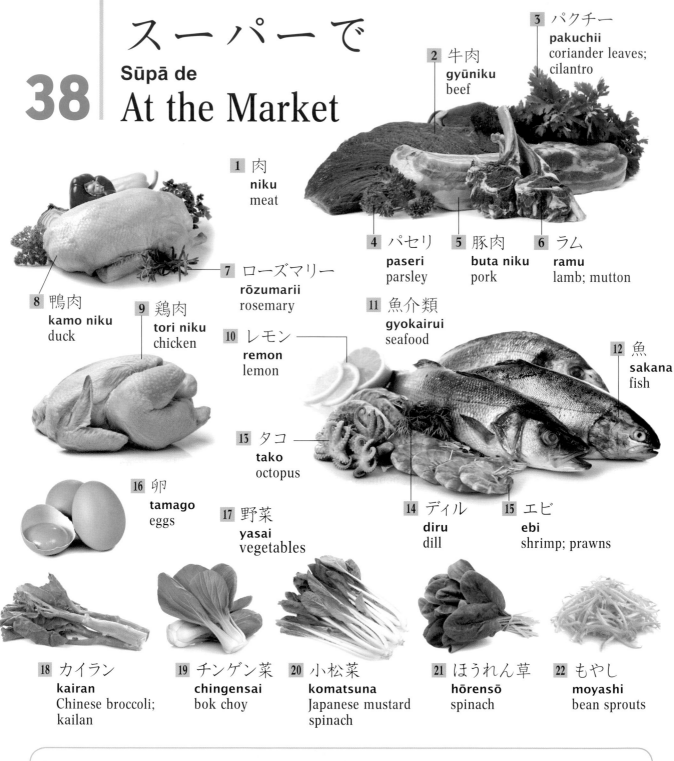

2 牛肉
gyūniku
beef

3 パクチー
pakuchii
coriander leaves;
cilantro

1 肉
niku
meat

4 パセリ
paseri
parsley

5 豚肉
buta niku
pork

6 ラム
ramu
lamb; mutton

7 ローズマリー
rōzumarii
rosemary

8 鴨肉
kamo niku
duck

9 鶏肉
tori niku
chicken

11 魚介類
gyokairui
seafood

10 レモン
remon
lemon

12 魚
sakana
fish

13 タコ
tako
octopus

16 卵
tamago
eggs

17 野菜
yasai
vegetables

14 ディル
diru
dill

15 エビ
ebi
shrimp; prawns

18 カイラン
kairan
Chinese broccoli;
kailan

19 チンゲン菜
chingensai
bok choy

20 小松菜
komatsuna
Japanese mustard
spinach

21 ほうれん草
hōrensō
spinach

22 もやし
moyashi
bean sprouts

59 私は近所の市場で食べ物を買っています。
Watashi wa kinjo no ichiba de tabemono o katte imasu.
I buy food at the local market.

60 そちらの野菜や肉のほうが新鮮です。しかもスーパーより安いです。
Sochira no yasai ya niku no hō ga shinsen desu. Shikamo sūpā yori yasui desu.
The vegetables and meat are very fresh there. And it is slightly cheaper than the supermarket.

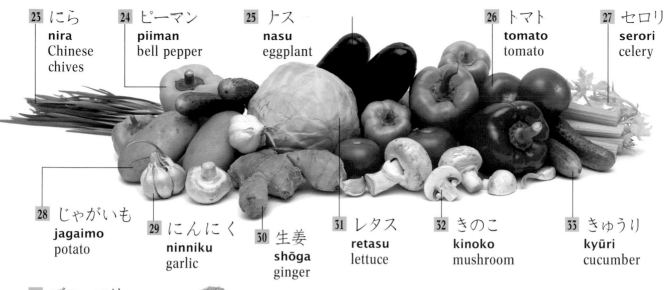

23 にら
nira
Chinese chives

24 ピーマン
piiman
bell pepper

25 ナス
nasu
eggplant

26 トマト
tomato
tomato

27 セロリ
serori
celery

28 じゃがいも
jagaimo
potato

29 にんにく
ninniku
garlic

30 生姜
shōga
ginger

31 レタス
retasu
lettuce

32 きのこ
kinoko
mushroom

33 きゅうり
kyūri
cucumber

34 ブロッコリー
burokkorii
broccoli

35 人参
ninjin
carrot

36 玉ねぎ
tamanegi
onion

37 唐辛子
tōgarashi
chili peppers

38 青ねぎ
aonegi
scallions;
spring onions

39 冬瓜
tōgan
winter melon

40 にが瓜; ゴーヤ
nigauri; gōya
bitter gourd

41 白菜
hakusai
Chinese cabbage

42 豆腐
tōfu
tofu

Additional Vocabulary

43 市場
ichiba
market

44 キャベツ
kyabetsu
cabbage

45 カリフラワー
karifurawā
cauliflower

46 インゲン
ingen
green beans;
string beans

47 カボチャ
kabocha
pumpkin

48 アスパラガス
asuparagasu
asparagus

49 ズッキーニ
zukkiini
zucchini

50 バジル
bajiru
basil

51 オレガノ
oregano
oregano

52 セージ
sēji
sage

53 タイム
taimu
thyme

54 タラゴン
taragon
tarragon

55 ひき肉
hikiniku
ground/minced
meat

56 豚ひき肉
buta hikiniku
ground/minced
pork

57 肉の種類
niku no shurui
types of meat

58 新鮮
shinsen
fresh

85

61 調味料
chōmiryō
seasonings

62 醤油
shōyu
soy sauce

63 ラー油
rāyu
hot chili oil

64 ゴマ油
goma abura
sesame oil

65 オリーブ油
oriibu oiru
olive oil

66 酢
su
vinegar

67 唐辛子粉
tōgarashiko
chili powder

68 味噌
miso
soybean paste

69 大豆
daizu
soybean

70 塩
shio
salt

71 七味
shichimi
seven spice

72 ふりかけ
furikake
seasonings sprinkled on rice

73 わさび
wasabi
wasabi

Additional Vocabulary

74 こしょう
koshō
pepper

75 砂糖
satō
sugar

76 みりん
mirin
cooking sweet wine

77 料理酒
ryōrishu
rice wine

78 米酢
komezu
rice vinegar

79 五香粉
ūshanfen; gokōfun
five-spice powder

80 でん粉; 片栗粉
denpun; katakuriko
starch

81 化学調味料
kagaku chōmiryō
monosodium glutamate (MSG)

82 カレー粉
karēko
curry powder

83 食用油;
サラダ油
**shokuyō abura;
saradayu**
cooking oil

84 ピーナッツオイル
piinattsu oiru
peanut oil

85 ココナッツ
オイル
kokonattsu oiru
coconut oil

86 パーム油; やし油
pāmuyu; yashiyu
palm oil

87 材料を揃えれば日本の料理は作りやすいです。
Zairyō o soroereba Nihon no ryōri wa tsukuriyasui desu.
Japanese food is easy to cook once you have all the ingredients.

English–Japanese Index

6 o'clock 六時 **rokuji** [15-4] *38*

100 yen 百円 **hyaku en** [9-5] *26*

1,000 yen 千円 **sen en** [9-12] *26*

10,000 yen 一万円 **ichiman en** [9-10] *26*

50 yen 五十円 **gojū en** [9-7] *26*

500 yen 五百円 **gohyaku en** [9-4] *26*

5,000 yen 五千円 **gosen en** [9-11] *26*

A

a banjo-like lute with three strings 三味線 **shamisen** [26-3] *60*

a brief moment 一瞬 **isshun** [15-33] *39*

a circle 円形 **enkei** [7-19] *23*

a day of the week 曜日 **yōbi** [16-3] *40*

a diamond (shape) ひし形 **hishigata** [7-28] *23*

a gentle breeze そよ風 **soyokaze** [17-6] *42*

a heart (shape) ハート型 **hātogata** [7-23] *23*

a hexagon 六角形 **rokkakkei** [7-27] *23*

a pentagon 五角形 **gokakkei** [7-21] *23*

a question; problem 問題 **mondai** [19-26] *47*

a rainbow 虹 **niji** [7-17] *22*

a rectangle 四角形 **shikakkei** [7-18] *23*

a square 正方形 **seihōkei** [7-22] *23*

a star (shape) 星型 **hoshigata** [7-25] *23*

a triangle 三角形 **sankakkei** [7-26] *23*

a trip; to travel 旅行 **ryokō** [31-17] *71*

a vertical bamboo flute 尺八 **shakuhachi** [26-5] *60*

abdomen 腹 **hara** [4-26] *17*

above 上 **ue** [13-4] *34*

accent アクセント **akusento** [21-14] *51*

accident 事故 **jiko** [27-34] *63*

according to によって **ni yotte** [23-44] *55*

account number 口座番号 **kōza bangō** [9-28] *27*

accountant 会計士 **kaikeishi** [25-5] *58*

actor; actress 俳優; 女優 **haiyū; joyū** [26-17] *61*

actually 実は **jitsu wa** [17-20] *43*

addition 足し算 **tashizan** [5-22] *19*

afraid 怖い **kowai** [29-33] *67*

Africa アフリカ **Afurika** [32-17] *73*

after school 放課後 **hōkago** [6-25] *20*

after that 後で **ato de** [23-45] *55*

air 空気 **kūki** [28-11] *64*

air conditioner エアコン **eakon** [3-13] *14*

air pollution 大気汚染 **taiki osen** [14-37] *37*

air quality 空気の質 **kūki no shitsu** [28-24] *65*

airplane 飛行機 **hikōki** [12-4] *32*

airport 空港 **kūkō** [11-1] *30*; [31-36] *71*

alarm clock 目覚し時計 **mezamashi-dokei** [15-12] *39*

algebra 代数 **daisū** [19-38] *47*

almonds アーモンド **āmondo** [37-24] *83*

alphabet アルファベット **arufabetto** [20-22] *49*

already すでに **sude ni** [13-59] *35*

also また **mata** [20-43] *49*

also; too それに **sore ni** [34-30] *77*

although のに **no ni** [28-38] *65*

altogether 全部で **zenbu de** [10-32] *29*

always いつも **itsumo** [25-35] *59*

ambulance 救急車 **kyūkyūsha** [27-21] *63*

America アメリカ **Amerika** [32-24] *73*

an octagon 八角形 **hakkakkei** [7-20] *23*

an oval だ円形 **daenkei** [7-24] *23*

Android phones アンドロイド 携帯 **Andoroido keitai** [24-7] *56*

ankle 足首 **ashikubi** [4-29] *17*

anniversary 記念日 **kinenbi** [18-29] *45*

another; other 他 **hoka** [31-45] *71*

Antarctica 南極 **Nankyoku** [32-20] *73*

antiseptic 消毒剤 **shōdokuzai** [27-36] *63*

anxious; worried 心配 **shinpai** [27-44] *63*

apartment アパート **apāto** [3-52] *14*; [11-13] *30*

apple りんご **ringo** [37-1] *82*

Apple (company) アップル **Appuru** [24-22] *57*

iPhones アイフォン **aifon** [24-8] *56*

apple pie アップルパイ **appuru pai** [35-11] *78*

application (computer program) アプリケーション **apurikēshon** [23-27] *55*

appointment 予約 **yoyaku** [27-20] *63*

apprentice 見習い **minarai** [25-27] *59*

April 四月 **shigatsu** [16-21] *41*

Arabic アラビア語 **Arabiago** [33-9] *74*

architect 建築家 **kenchikuka** [25-9] *58*

area code 市外局番 **shigai kyokuban** [24-33] *56*

arm 腕 **ude** [4-19] *17*

art museum 美術館 **bijutsukan** [11-14] *31*

artery 動脈 **dōmyaku** [4-45] *17*

artist 芸術家 **geijutsuka** [25-7] *58*

as a result of of から **kara** [28-39] *65*

Asia アジア **Ajia** [32-18] *73*

asparagus アスパラガス **asuparagasu** [38-48] *85*

assignment 課題 **kadaiv** [19-32] *47*; 宿題 **shukudai** [21-27] *51*

attend a birthday party 誕生会 へ行く **tanjōkai e iku** [18-26] *45*

attic; loft 屋根裏 **yaneura** [3-54] *14*

audience 観客 **kankyaku** [26-14] *61*

auditorium 講堂 **kōdō** [20-19] *49*

aunt おばさん **obasan** [2-17] *13*

August 八月 **hachigatsu** [16-25] *41*

Australia オーストラリア **Ōsutoraria** [32-27] *73*

autumn/fall 秋 **aki** [17-3] *42*

B

bacon ベーコン **bēkon** [35-20] *79*

bad 悪い **warui** [8-7] *24*

bad weather 悪い天気 **warui tenki** [14-35] *37*

badminton バドミントン **badominton** [30-5] *68*

baguette フランスパン **furansupan** [35-6] *78*

balcony バルコニー **barukonii** [3-2] *14*

ball ボール **bōru** [30-27] *69*

ball-shaped snack with octopus たこ焼き **takoyaki** [34-24] *77*

banana バナナ **banana** [37-7] *82*

band; orchestra 楽団 **gakudan** [26-28] *61*

bandage 包帯 **hōtai** [27-53] *63*

bank 銀行 **ginkō** [11-7] *30*

bank deposit 預金 **yokin** [9-27] *27*

barbecue バーベキュー **bābekyū** [35-31] *79*

barley 大麦 **ōmugi** [37-35] *83*

baseball 野球 **yakyū** [30-7] *68*

basement; cellar 地下 **chika** [3-55] *14*

basil バジル **bajiru** [38-50] *85*

basketball バスケットボール **basukettobōru** [30-24] *69*

bathroom 浴室 **yokushitsu** [3-37] *15*

bathtub; 浴槽 **ofuro; yokusō** [3-42] *15*

beach 海; 浜 **umi; hama** [31-33] *71*

bean sprouts もやし **moyashi** [38-22] *84*

beans 豆 **mame** [37-45] *83*

bear 熊 **kuma** [29-6] *66*

because だから; なので **dakara; nanode** [23-46] *55*

bed ベッド **beddo** [3-20] *14*

bedroom 寝室 **shinshitsu** [3-21] *14*

bee; honeybee 蜂; 蜜蜂 **hachi; mitsubachi** [29-26] *67*

beef 牛肉 **gyūniku** [38-2] *84*

beer ビール **biiru** [36-26] *81*

before 前 **mae** [15-31] *39*

beginning of spring 節分 **Setsubun** [18-5] *44*

behind 後ろ **ushiro** [8-21] *25*; [13-15] *34*

bell pepper ピーマン **piiman** [38-24] *85*

below 下 **shita** [13-5] *34*

belt ベルト **beruto** [10-19] *29*

between; among 間 **aida** [15-32] *39*

beverage 飲み物 **nomimono** [36-1] *80*

bicycle 自転車 **jitensha** [12-18] *33*; [30-11] *68*

big 大きい **ōkii** [8-11] *25*

bill; invoice 会計 **kaikei** [10-40] *29*

biology 生物学 **seibutsugaku** [19-41] *47*

bird 鳥 **tori** [29-20] *67*

birthday 誕生日 **tanjōbi** [18-25] *45*

bitter gourd にが瓜; ゴーヤ **nigauri; gōya** [38-40] *85*

black 黒 **kuro** [7-4] *22*

Black Friday ブラックフライデー **burakku furaidē** [10-21] *29*

blackboard 黒板 **kokuban** [20-2] *48*

blog ブログ **burogu** [23-36] *55*

blood 血; 血液 **chi; ketsueki** [4-42] *17*

blood pressure 血圧 **ketsuatsu** [27-9] *62*

blood test 血液検査 **ketsueki kensa** [27-7] *62*

blouse ブラウス **burausu** [10-7] *28*

blue 青 **ao** [7-6] *22*

boarding pass 搭乗券 **tōjōken** [31-9] *70*

bok choy チンゲン菜 **chingensai** [38-19] *84*

bone 骨 **hone** [4-44] *17*

book 本 **hon** [19-7] *46*

book shelf 本棚 **hondana** [3-35] *15*

books, notes 一冊、二冊、三冊 ... **issatsu, nisatsu, sansatsu ...** [22-10] *52*

boots 長靴 **nagagutsu** [14-3] *36*

bottle ボトル **botoru** [36-32] *81*

boutique ブティック **butikku** [10-24] *29*

bowl 茶碗 **chawan** [34-9] *76*

brain 脳 **nō** [4-30] *17*

bread パン **pan** [34-7] *76*

bridge 橋 **hashi** [11-27] *31*

broccoli ブロッコリー **burokkorii** [38-34] *85*

brother-in-law 義理の兄弟 **giri no kyōdai** [2-33] *12*

brothers 兄弟 **tomodachi** [2-12] *13*

brown 茶色 **chairo** [7-9] *22*

browser ブラウザ **burauza** [23-37] *55*

Brunei ブルネイ **Burunei** [32-9] *72*

buckwheat; buckwheat noodles そば **soba** [37-37] *83*; [34-17] *77*

bullet train 新幹線 **shinkansen** [12-8] *32*

bus route バス路線 **basu rosen** [12-32] *33*

bus stop バス停 **basutei** [12-13] *33*

business district ビジネス街 **bijinesugai** [11-24] *31*

busy 忙しい **isogashii** [8-8] *24*

but; however でも; しかし **demo; shikashi** [28-36] *65*

butter; cream バター; クリーム **batā; kuriimu** [35-24] *79*

butterfly 蝶 **chō** [29-27] *67*

by bus; to take a bus バスで **basu de** [12-21] *33*

by train; to take a train 電車で **densha de** [12-23] *33*

C

cabbage キャベツ **kyabetsu** [38-44] *85*

cabinet 戸棚 **todana** [3-25] *15*

cable network ケーブルネットワーク **kēburu nettowāku** [23-43] *55*

cake ケーキ **kēki** [35-23] *79*

calculator 計算機; 電卓 **keisanki; dentaku** [5-16] *19*; [20-10] *48*

calculus 微積分 **bisekibun** [19-42] *47*

calendar カレンダー **karendā** [16-1] *40*

calligraphy 書道 **shodō** [21-5] *50*

Cambodia カンボジア **Kanbojia** [32-7] *72*

camera カメラ **kamera** [31-15] *70*

can; to be able to できる **dekiru** [28-33] *65*

cantaloupe マスクメロン **masukumeron** [37-17] *82*

car 車 **kuruma** [12-1] *32*

carpet 絨毯 **jūtan** [3-12] *14*

carrot 人参 **ninjin** [38-35] *85*

cash 現金 **genkin** [9-32] *27*

cashew nuts カシューナッツ **kashū nattsu** [37-29] *83*

cashier レジ **reji** [10-26] *29*

cat 猫 **neko** [29-22] *67*

cauliflower カリフラワー **karifurawā** [38-45] *85*

CD; DVD CD; DVD **shiidii; diibuidii** [23-12] *54*

ceiling 天井 **tenjō** [3-4] *14*

celery セロリ **serori** [38-27] *85*

cello チェロ **chero** [26-18] *61*

century (100 years) 世紀 **seiki** [16-39] *41*

cereal シリアル **shiriaru** [35-25] *79*

certainly 必ず **kanarazu** [10-33] *29*

chair 椅子 **isu** [3-8] *14*

Champagne シャンパン **Shanpan** [36-22] *81*

changes 変化 **henka** [28-30] *65*

chat room チャットルーム **chatto rūmu** [23-33] *55*

cheap 安い **yasui** [9-22] *27*

check 小切手 **kogitte** [9-13] *27*

cheek 頬 **hoho** [4-4] *16*

cheese チーズ **chiizu** [35-24] *79*

chef; cook シェフ; コック **shefu; kokku** [25-11] *59*; [34-3] *76*

chemistry 化学 **kagaku** [19-40] *47*

chest 胸 **mune** [4-25] *17*

chestnuts 栗 **kuri** [37-26] *83*

chicken 鶏 **niwatori** [29-19] *67*; 鶏肉 **tori niku** [38-9] *84*

children 子ども **kodomo** [2-4] *12*

Children's Day 子供の日 **Kodomo no hi** [18-6] *44*

chili peppers 唐辛子 **tōgarashi** [38-37] *85*

chili powder 唐辛子粉 **tōgarashiko** [38-67] *86*

chin 顎 **ago** [4-13] *16*

China 中国 **Chūgoku** [32-23] *73*

Chinese (language) 中国語 **Chūgokugo** [33-19] *75*

Chinese broccoli; kailan カイラン **kairan** [38-18] *84*

Chinese cabbage 白菜 **hakusaii** [38-41] *85*

Chinese chives にら **nira** [38-23] *85*

Chinese character 漢字 **kanji** [21-6] *51*

Chinese reading 音読み **on-yomi** [21-7] *51*

Chinese rice wine 紹興酒 **shōkōshu** [36-24] *81*

chocolates チョコレート **chokorēto** [18-16] *45*

choice 選択 **sentaku** [34-28] *77*

chopsticks 箸 **hashi** [34-8] *76*

Christmas クリスマス **kurisumasu** [18-23] *45*

church 教会 **kyōkai** [11-32] *31*

city 都会; 街 **tokai; machi** [11-11] *30*

classmates 同級生; クラスメート **dōkyūsei; kurasumēto** [20-15] *48*

classroom 教室 **kyōshitsu** [20-4] *48*

clean きれい **kirei** [28-18] *65*; 清潔 **seiketsu** [28-27] *65*

clean energy クリーンエネルギー **kuriin enerugii** [28-21] *65*

clear (sky) 晴れ **hare** [14-4] *36*

clear day 晴れた日 **hareta hi** [14-5] *36*

clock 時計 **tokei** [15-6] *38*

clothes 服 **fuku** [10-6] *28*

clothing size 洋服のサイズ **yōfuku no saizu** [7-29] *23*

cloud 雲 **kumo** [14-24] *37*

cloudy day 曇った日 **kumotta hi** [14-7] *36*

coal 石炭 **sekitan** [28-23] *65*

coat or jacket コート **kōto** [14-18] *37*

cocktails カクテル **kakuteru** [36-18] *81*

coconut ココナッツ **kokonattsu** [37-6] *82*

coconut oil ココナッツオイル **kokonattsu oiru** [38-85] *86*

coffee コーヒー **kōhii** [35-19] *79*; [36-6] *80*

coffee table コーヒーテーブル **kōhi tēburu** [3-11] *14*

coin, money お金 **okane** [9-17] *27*

coins 硬貨 **kōka** [9-3] *26*

cola コーラ **kōra** [36-10] *80*

cold 寒い **samui** [14-22] *37*

cold day 寒い日 **samui hi** [14-23] *37*

cold water 冷たい水 **tsumetai mizu** [36-30] *81*

colleague 同僚 **dōryō** [25-24] *59*

color 色 **iro** [7-1] *22*

Coming of Age Day 成人の日 **Seijin no hi** [18-4] *44*

company 会社 **kaisha** [25-20] *59*

competition; game 競技会; 試合 **kyōgikai; shiai** [30-13] *69*

computer lab コンピューターラボ **konpyūtā rabo** [20-20] *49*

computers コンピューター **konpyūtā** [23-1] *54*

concert コンサート **konsāto** [26-13] *61*

conference center 会館 **kaikan** [11-8] *30*

conscientious; serious 真面目 **majime** [19-46] *47*

Constitution Day 憲法記念日 **Kenpō kinenbi** [18-21] *45*

cooking oil 食用油; サラダ油 **shokuyō abura; saradayu** [38-83] *86*

cooked rice ご飯 **gohan** [34-5] *76*

cooker hood レンジフード **renji hūdo** [3-28] *15*

cooking sweet wine みりん **mirin** [38-76] *86*

coriander leaves; cilantro パクチー **pakuchii** [38-3] *84*

corn とうもろこし **tōmorokoshi** [37-46] *83*

cosmetics 化粧品 **keshōhin** [10-17] *29*

cousins いとこ **itoko** [2-24] *13*

Countries in Southeast Asia 東南アジア諸国 **Tōnan Ajia shokoku** [32-1] *72*

country code 国番号 **kuni bangō** [24-32] *56*

course; academic program コース **kōsu** [21-26] *51*

cow 牛 **ushi** [29-13] *67*

crackers クラッカー **kurakkā** [37-42] *83*

cram school 塾 **juku** [20-39] *49*

credit card クレジットカード **kurejitto kādo** [9-15] *27*; [10-30] *29*

crops 作物 **sakumotsu** [17-17] *43*

cruise center 客船案内所 **kyakusen annaisho** [31-37] *71*

cruise ship 客船 **kyakusen** [31-13] *70*

cucumber きゅうり **kyūri** [38-33] *85*

culture 文化 **bunka** [21-21] *51*

Culture Day 文化の日 **Bunka no hiv** [18-10] *44*

cups and glasses of drink; spoonful 一杯、二杯、三杯 **ippai, nipai, sanpai …** [22-6] *52*

currency 通貨 **tsūka** [31-21] *71*

currency exchange 為替 **kawase** [9-17] *27*

curry powder カレー粉 **karēko** [38-82] *86*

curtain カーテン **kāten** [3-17] *14*

customs 税関 **zeikan** [31-27] *71*

cute; adorable 可愛い **kawaii** [29-34] *67*

D

dance (performance art) 舞踊 **buyō** [26-21] *61*

dark color 濃い **koi** [7-15] *22*

daughter 娘 **musume** [2-5] *12*

daughter-in-law 嫁; 義理の娘 **yome; giri no musume** [2-29] *12*

day after tomorrow 明後日 **asatte** [16-10] *40*

day before yesterday 一昨日 **ototoi** [16-6] *40*

day of a month 日 **nichi** [16-5] *40*

debt 借金 **shakkin** [9-26] *27*

decade (10 years) 十年 **jūnen** [16-38] *41*

December 十二月 **jūnigatsu** [16-29] *41*

decision 決定 **kettei** [10-36] *29*

delivery van 配送トラック **haisō torakku** [12-7] *32*

dentist 歯医者 **haisha** [25-14] *59*

dentistry 歯科 **shika** [27-22] *63*

department store デパート **depāto** [10-23] *29*

dermatology 皮膚科 **hifuka** [27-24] *63*

desk 机 **tsukue** [3-36] *15*

desktop computer デスクトップ・コンピューター **desukutoppu konpyūtā** [23-4] *54*

diary 日記 **nikki** [16-45] *41*

dictionary 辞書 **jisho** [19-11] *46*

diet drinks ダイエットドリンク **daietto dorinku** [36-15] *80*

difficult 難しい **muzukashii** [8-15] *25*; [21-32] *51*

digestive system 消化器系 **shōkakikei** [4-37] *17*

digits; number 桁数 **ketasū** [5-29] *19*

dill ディル **diru** [38-14] *84*

dinosaur 恐竜 **kyōryū** [29-10] *66*

direction 方向 **hōkō** [13-36] *35*

discount 割引 **waribiki** [9-21] *27*

distance 距離 **kyori** [13-37] *35*

distilled spirits 焼酎 **shōchū** [36-25] *81*

division 割り算 **warizan** [5-26] *19*

doctor 医者 **isha** [27-4] *62*

doctor's consultation room 診察室 **shinsatsushitsu** [27-18] *62*

dog 犬 **inu** [29-21] *67*

Doll Festival ひな祭り **Hinamatsuri** [18-33] *45*

donuts ドーナッツ **dōnattsu** [35-5] *78*

door ドア **doa** [3-46] *15*

down 下 **shita** [8-1] *24*

downtown 中心部 **chūshinbu** [11-23] *31*

dragon 竜; 龍 **tatsu; ryū** [29-23] *67*

drawer 引き出し **hikidashi** [3-34] *15*

dried fruits ドライフルーツ **dorai furūtsu** [37-44] *83*

driver 運転手 **untenshu** [12-3] *32*

drums ドラム **doramu** [26-7] *60*

duck 鴨肉 **kamo niku** [38-8] *84*

E

ear 耳 mimi [4-2] 16

ear, nose, and throat 耳鼻科 jibika [27-25] 63

early 早い hayai [15-27] 39

early morning 早朝 sōchō [15-21] 39

earphones イヤホン iyahon [26-26] 61

earth; ground 地面; 大地 jimen; daichi [28-31] 65

east 東 higashi [13-10] 34

East Timor 東ティモール Higashi Timōru [32-12] 72

Easter 復活祭 fukkatsusai [18-20] 45

easy 優しい ryasashii [8-15] 25; 易しい yasashii [21-31] 51

economics 経済学 keizaigaku [19-37] 47

eggplant ナス nasu [38-25] 85

eggs 卵 tamago [38-16] 84

eight 八 hachi [5-8] 18

elbow 肘 hiji [4-20] 17

electric car 電気自動車 denki jidōsha [28-6] 64

electric socket; power point コンセント konsento [3-50] 14

elementary school 小学校 shōgakkō [20-31] 49

elephant 象 zō [29-14] 67

elevator エレベーター erebētā [3-45] 15

email 電子メール denshi mēru [23-15] 54

emergency 救急 kyūkyū [27-39] 63

emergency room 救急救命室 kyūkyū-kyūmeishitsu [27-2] 62

Emperor's Birthday 天皇誕生日 Tennō tanjōbi [18-34] 45

energy drinks 栄養ドリンク eiyō dorinku [36-70] 80

engineer エンジニア enjinia [25-4] 58

English 英語 Eigo [33-1] 74

enter 入る hairu [8-6] 24

enthusiastic 熱心な nesshin na [2-38] 12

entrance 玄関 genkan [3-57] 14

entrepreneur 企業家 kigyōka [25-21] 59

environment 環境 kankyō [28-28] 65

equal イコール ikōru [5-21] 19

eraser 消しゴム keshigomu [19-14] 47

Europe ヨーロッパ Yōroppa [32-16] 73

even numbers 偶数 gūsū [5-26] 19

Everybody eats together 皆で食事をする Minna de shokuji o suru [6-14] 21

exams 試験; テスト shiken; tesuto [19-1] 46

Excuse me ... (call a waiter/waitress) すみません Sumimasen [34-36] 77

exercise book 練習帳 renshūchō [21-28] 51

exit 出る deru [8-6] 24

expensive 高い takai [9-23] 27

expressway 高速道路 kōsoku dōro [11-18] 31

eye 目 me [4-8] 16

eyebrow 眉毛 mayuge [4-7] 16

F

face 顔 kao [4-5] 16

Facebook フェイスブック Feisubukku [24-18] 57

fake 偽物 nisemono [8-27] 25

family 家族 kazoku [2-35] 12

famous 有名 yūmei [26-31] 61

fan 扇子 sensu [17-14] 43

far 遠い tōi [8-25] 25; [13-43] 35

farmer 農家 nōka [25-19] 59

fast 速い hayai [8-28] 25

fat 太っています futotte imasu [8-13] 25

father お父さん otōsan [2-13] 13

Father's Day 父の日 Chichi no hi [18-13] 44

February 二月 nigatsu [16-19] 41

female 女性 josei [2-3] 12

festival, holiday 祝日; 祭日 shukujitsu; saijitsu [18-1] 44

fever 熱 netsu [27-12] 62

few 少し sukoshi [8-3] 24

fifteen minutes to seven; a quarter to seven 六時四十五分; 七時十五分前 rokuji yonjūgo-fun; shichiji jūgofun mae [15-10] 38

fifteen minutes past six; a quarter past six 六時十五分 rokuji jūgofun [15-8] 38

file ファイル fairu [23-22] 55

finally ようやく yōyaku [15-36] 39

financier 投資家 tōshika [25-3] 58

fingers 指 yubi [4-15] 16

finish line ゴール gōru [30-14] 69

fire engine 消防車 shōbōsha [12-16] 33

firefighter 消防士 shōbōshi [25-18] 59

fireworks 花火 hanabi [18-3] 44

first aid kit 救急箱 kyūkyū-bako [27-52] 63

fish 魚 sakana [29-28] 67; [38-12] 84

five 五 go [5-5] 18

five minutes past six 六時五分 rokuji gofun [15-5] 38

five minutes to seven 七時五十五分; 七時五分前 roku-ji gojūgo-fun; shichi-ji go-fun mae [15-11] 38

five yen 五円 go en [9-8] 26

five-spice powder 五香粉 ūshanfen; gokōfun [38-79] 86

floor 床 yuka [3-16] 14

floors of a building 階 kai/gai [22-11] 53

flour 小麦粉 komugiko [37-47] 83

flower 花 hana [28-2] 64

flute フルート furūto [26-10] 60

fog 霧 kiri [14-25] 37

foot 足 ashi [4-22] 17

foot (measurement) フィート fiito [13-41] 35

for the purpose of ... のために ... no tame ni [28-32] 65

forehead 額 hitai [4-17] 17

forest 森 mori [28-13] 65

former 前の mae no [17-19] 43

fork フォーク fōku [34-12] 76

four 四 yon; shi [5-4] 18

four seasons 四季 shiki [17-18] 43

French フランス語 Furansugo [33-2] 74

free wifi 無料Wi-Fi muryō waifai [31-31] 71

french fries ポテトフライ potetofurai [35-28] 79

frequently よく yoku [15-19] 39

fresh 新鮮 shinsen [38-58] 85

freshman year in college 大学一年生 daigaku ichinensei [20-35] 49

Friday 金曜日 Kin'yōbi [16-16] 40

fried dumplings 餃子 gyōza [34-15] 77

fried rice チャーハン chāhan [34-6] 76

friends 友達 tomodachi [1-40] 11

fruit juice フルーツジュース furūtsu jūsu [36-3] 80

G

garage 車庫 shako [3-56] 14

garbage truck ゴミ収集車 gomi shūshūsha [12-6] 32

garden 庭園; 庭 teien; niwa [28-1] 64

garlic にんにく ninniku [38-29] 85

gas station; petrol station ガソリンスタンド gasorin sutando [11-6] 30

gathering; meeting ミーティング miitingu [1-19] 11

general medicine 内科 naika [27-23] 63

general object counter 一つ、二つ、三つ … hitotsu, futatsu, mittsu … [22-1] 52

general surgery 外科 geka [27-24] 63

generally 一般 ippan [10-34] 29

geography 地理 chiri [19-43] 47

geometry 幾何学 kikagaku [19-34] 47

German ドイツ語 Doitsugo [33-4] 74

gift 贈り物; プレゼン okuri-mono; purezento [18-22] 45

ginger 生姜 shōga [38-30] 85

giraffe キリン kirin [29-3] 66

give あげる ageru [8-2] 24

glass; cup コップ; カップ koppu; kappu [36-33] 81

glasses, spectacles メガネ megane [10-11] 28

globe 地球 chikyū [32-28] 73

gloves 手袋 tebukuro [14-31] 37

go faster もっと速く motto hayaku [12-27] 33

go straight まっすぐ行ってください massugu itte kudasai [12-29] 33

goat ヤギ yagi [29-11] 67

Golden Week ゴールデンウィーク Gōruden wiiku [18-31] 45

gold 金色 kin'iro [7-13] 22

golf ゴルフ gorufu [30-15] 69

good 良い yoi [8-7] 24

good weather 良い天気 yoi tenki [14-34] 37

Google グーグル Gūguru [24-19] 57

gorilla ゴリラ gorira [29-8] 66

grade; class 級 kyū [19-22] 47

grades 成績 seiseki [20-23] 49

grains; cereal 穀物 kokumotsu [37-40] 83

grammar 文法 bunpō [21-22] 51

grandfather おじいさん ojiisan [2-7] 13

grandmother おばあさん obāsan [2-8] 13

grandson; granddaughter 孫; 孫娘 mago; mago-musume [2-30] 12

grapes ぶどう budō [37-16] 82

grass 草 kusa [28-5] 64

gray 灰色 haiiro [7-10] 22

great; wonderful; terrible すごい sugoi [29-32] 67

great grandfather 曾おじいさん hii ojiisan [2-9] 13

great grandmother 曾おばあさん hii obāsan [2-10] 13

Greek ギリシャ語 Girishago [33-10] 75

green 緑 midori [7-7] 22

green beans; string beans インゲン ingen [38-46] 85

ground/minced meat ひき肉 hikiniku [38-55] 85

ground/minced pork 豚ひき肉 buta hikiniku [38-56] 85

grove 林 hayashi [28-14] 65

guest; customer お客さん okyakusan [1-20] 11

guesthouse; lodge 民宿 minshuku [31-38] 71

guitar ギター gitā [26-1] 60

gym フィットネスジム fittonesu jimu [11-19] 31

gynecology 産婦人科 sanfujinka [27-27] 63

H

hail 霰 arare [14-29] 37

hair 髪 kami [4-6] 16

half past six 六時半 rokuji han [15-9] 38

Halloween ハロウィーン Harowiin [18-19] 45

ham ハム hamu [35-12] 78

hamburger ハンバーガー hanbāgā [35-27] 79

hand 手 te [4-18] 17

happy 嬉しい ureshii [1-10] 10; 嬉しい ureshii [8-31] 25

harvest 収穫 shūkaku [17-13] 43

hat 帽子 bōshi [10-16] 28; [14-30] 37

hazel nuts ヘーゼルナッツ hēzeru nattsu [37-27] 83

head 頭 atama [4-1] 16

health 健康 kenkō [4-47] 17

Health and Sports Day 体育の日 Taiiku no hi [18-8] 44

healthy 健康 kenkō [30-28] 69

heart 心臓 shinzō [4-32] 17

Hebrew ヘブライ語 Heburaigo [33-11] 75

here ここ koko [13-2] 34

high 高い takai [8-29] 25

highlighter 蛍光ペン keikōpen [19-19] 47

Hindi ヒンディー語 Hindiigo [33-13] 75

history 歴史 rekishi [19-29] 47

hobby 趣味 shumi [26-30] 61

home; house 家 ie; uchi [3-51] 14; [11-26] 31
home delivery 宅配 takuhai [10-27] 29
homework 宿題 shukudai [19-27] 47
Honda ホンダ Honda [24-21] 57
hope 希望 kibō [27-49] 63
horse 馬 uma [29-15] 67
horse carriage 馬車 basha [12-33] 33
hospital 病院 byōin [27-1] 62
hot 暑い atsui [14-20] 37
hot chili oil ラー油 rāyu [38-63] 86
hot day 暑い日 atsui hi [14-21] 37
hot dog ホットドッグ hotto doggu [35-1] 78
hot water お湯 oyu [36-29] 81
hotel ホテル hoteru [11-2] 30; [11-20] 31; [31-1] 70
hotel reservation ホテルの予約 hoteru no yoyaku [31-20] 71
hour(s) 時 ji [15-1] 38; 時間 jikan [22-20] 53
hours of the day 時 ji [22-19] 53
housefly ハエ hae [29-25] 67
How are things? どうですか? Dō desu ka? [1-38] 11
how much (time/distance) どのくらい dono kurai [13-56] 35
hungry お腹が空いています onaka ga suite imasu [8-22] 25
hurricane ハリケーン harikēn [14-38] 37
hurts 痛い itai [27-40] 63
husband 夫 otto [2-27] 12
husband and wife 夫婦 fūfu [2-14] 13

I

I; me 私 watashi [2-20] 13
ice cream アイスクリーム aisu kuriimu [35-7] 78
ice cube 氷; アイスキューブ kōri; aisu kyūbu [36-31] 81
ice-skating アイススケート aisu sukēto [30-16] 69
iced tea アイスティー aisu tii [36-8] 80
idiom 熟語 jukugo [21-15] 51
idle 暇 hima [8-8] 24
illness 病気 byōki [4-48] 17
important 重要な jūyō na [27-50] 63
in a moment じきに jiki ni [15-34] 39
in addition しかも shikamo [23-47] 55
in front 前 mae [8-21] 25; [13-14] 34
in the afternoon; p.m. 下午 gogo [15-24] 39
in the morning; a.m. 午前 gozen [15-22] 39
index 指標 shihyō [28-25] 65
India インド Indo [32-25] 73
Indonesia インドネシア Indoneshia [32-11] 72
Indonesian インドネシア語 Indoneshiago [33-14] 75
injection 注射 chūsha [27-7] 62
inside 中 naka [8-20] 25; 内側 uchigawa [13-34] 35

installment (payment) 掛け金 kakekin [9-30] 27
intelligent; clever 賢い kashikoi [20-24] 49
interest 利子 rishi [9-24] 27
intern インターン intān [25-28] 59
Internet access インターネットアクセス intānetto akusesu [23-28] 55
internet cafes ネットカフェ netto kafe [24-4] 56
Internet language インターネット言語 intānetto gengo [24-26] 56
Internet slang インターネットスラング intānetto surangu [24-28] 56
intestines 腸 chō [4-34] 17
introduce yourself 自己紹介する jikoshōkai suru [1-14] 11
Italy イタリア Itaria [32-26] 73
Italian イタリア語 Itariago [33-5] 74

J

January 一月 ichigatsu [16-18] 41
Japan 日本 Nihon; Nippon [32-21] 73
Japanese language 日本語 Nihongo [21-12] 51; [33-8] 74
Japanese mustard spinach 小松菜 komatsuna [38-20] 84
Japanese reading 訓読み kun-yomi [21-8] 51
Japanese traditional cakes 和菓子 wagashi [18-12] 44
jeans ジーンズ jiinzu [10-9] 28
joyful 幸せ shiawase [1-11] 10
judge 裁判官 saibankan [25-2] 58
juice ジュース jūsu [35-18] 79
July 七月 shichigatsu [16-24] 41
June 六月 rokugatsu [16-23] 41
junior year in college 大学三年生 daigaku sannensei [20-37] 49

K

Kabuki theater 歌舞伎 Kabuki [26-16] 61
karaoke カラオケ karaoke [26-11] 61
ketchup; tomato sauce ケチャップ kechappu [35-36] 79
kettle やかん yakan [3-29] 15
keyboard キーボード kiibōdo [23-5] 54
keys 鍵 kagi [3-5] 14
kidneys 腎臓 jinzō [4-33] 17
kilometer キロ kiro [13-38] 35; [22-14] 53
kilograms キロ kiro [22-14] 53
kitchen 台所 daidokoro [3-23] 15
knee 膝 hiza [4-21] 17
knife ナイフ naifu [34-13] 76
Korea 韓国 Kankoku [32-22] 73
Korean 韓国語 Kankokugo [33-16] 75

L

L size エルサイズ eru saizu [7-32] 23
laboratory 研究室 kenkyushitsu [20-21] 49
laboratory test 実験 jikken [27-8] 62
lamb; mutton ラム ramu [38-6] 84

lamp ランプ Rampu [3-7] 14
Laos ラオス Raosu [32-6] 72
laptop ラップトップ rapputoppu [23-6] 54
large 大きい ōkii [7-35] 23
large animals 一頭、二頭、三頭 … ittō, nitō, santō … [22-8] 52
larger もっと大きい motto ōkii [7-40] 23
lasagne ラザニア razania [35-9] 78
last month 先月 sengetsu [16-42] 41
last week 先週 senshū [16-41] 41
last year 去年 kyonen [16-30] 41
late 遅い osoi [15-28] 39
later 後で ato de [15-30] 39
lawyer 弁護士 bengoshi [25-1] 58
leap year 閏年 urūdoshi [16-37] 41
lecture hall 講義室 kōgishitsu [20-13] 48
left side 左側 hidarigawa [13-29] 35
leg 脚 ashi [4-28] 17
leisure 暇 hima [6-34] 20
lemon レモン remon [37-11] 82; [38-10] 84
lesson レッスン ressun [21-25] 51
letter 手紙 tegami [19-12] 46
lettuce レタス retasu [38-31] 85
level (of achievement) 水準 suijun [19-47] 47
library 図書館 toshokan [20-3] 48
light color 薄い usui [7-16] 22
light switch 電気のスイッチ denki no suitchi [3-49] 14
lightning 稲妻 inazuma [14-12] 36
lime ライム raimu [37-12] 82
LINE ライン Rain [24-6] 56
linguistics 語学 gogaku [21-24] 51
lion ライオン raion [29-5] 66
lips 唇 kuchibiru [4-14] 16
literature 文学 bungaku [19-28] 47
liver 肝臓 kanzō [4-35] 17
living room 居間 ima [3-1] 14
loan; credit ローン rōn [9-25] 27
long 長い nagai [8-9] 24
long, cylindrical object counter: like pencils, flowers, and trees 一本、二本、三本 … ippon, nihon, sanbon … [22-4] 52
long distance call 市外電話 shigai denwa [24-31] 56
long zither with 13 strings 琴 koto [26-2] 60
long-distance running 長距離走 chōkyorisō [30-10] 68
longan リュウガン ryūgan [37-14] 82
low 低い hikui [8-29] 25
luggage 荷物 nimotsu [31-4] 70
lungs 肺 hai [4-31] 17
lychee ライチ raiche [37-13] 82

M

M size エムサイズ emu saizu [7-34] 23

macadamia nuts マカデミアナッツ makademia nattsu [37-25] 83
machines: like cars and computers 一台、二台、三台 … ichidai, nidai, sandai … [22-5] 52
magazine 雑誌 zasshi [19-10] 46
Malaysia マレーシア Marēshia [32-8] 72
main 主な omo na [27-51] 63
male 男性 dansei [2-2] 12
manager 管理職 kanrishoku [25-16] 58
mandarin orange みかん mikan [37-4] 82
mango マンゴー mangō [37-2] 82
many たくさん takusan [8-3] 24
map 地図 chizu [31-2] 70
March 三月 sangatsu [16-20] 41
marker pen マーカー mākā [19-15] 47
market 市場 ichiba [38-43] 85
mashed potatoes マッシュポテト masshu poteto [35-14] 78
mask マスク具 masuku [28-29] 65
mathematics 数学 sūgaku [19-4] 46
May 五月 gogatsu [16-22] 41
maybe かもしれない kamoshirenai [31-47] 71
meat 肉 niku [38-1] 84
medicine 薬 kusuri [27-15] 62
medium (size) 中ぐらい chūgurai [7-36] 23
meaning 意味 imi [21-9] 51
meter メートル mētoru [13-40] 35
method 方法 hōhō [25-32] 59
menu メニュー menyū [34-4] 76
Microsoft マイクロソフト Maikurosofuto [24-23] 57
microwave oven 電子レンジ denshi renji [3-24] 15
middle; center 間 aida [13-28] 35
middle school 中学校 chūgakkō [20-32] 49
midnight 真夜中 mayonaka [15-25] 39
mile(s) マイル mairu [13-39] 35; [22-15] 53
millennium (1,000 years) 千年 sennen [16-40] 41
millet キビ kibi [37-36] 83
milk 牛乳 gyūnyū [36-5] 80
mineral water ミネラルウォーター mineraru wōtā [36-2] 80
minute(s) 分 fun [15-2] 38; fun; pun [22-18] 53
mobile phone 携帯電話 keitai denwa [24-9] 56
Monday 月曜日 Getsuyōbi [16-12] 40
monkey 猿 saru [29-7] 66
monosodium glutamate (MSG) 化学調味料 kagaku chōmiryō [38-81] 86
month 月 gatsu; getsu [16-2] 40
months ヶ月 kagetsu [22-22] 53
monument 記念碑 kinenhi [11-31] 31; [31-34] 71
moon 月 tsuki [14-27] 37
more; even more もっと motto [10-35] 29

mosquito 蚊 ka [29-24] 67

mother お母さん okāsan [2-15] 13

Mother's Day 母の日 Haha no hi [18-14] 44

motorcycle バイク; オートバイ baiku; ōtobai [12-9] 32

mountain climbing 山登り yamanobori [30-4] 68

mouse マウス mausu [23-10] 54

mousepad マウスパッド mausupaddo [23-9] 54

mouth 口 kuchi [4-10] 16

movie theater 映画館 eigakan [11-21] 31

multimedia マルチメディア maruchimedia [23-35] 55

multiplication 掛け算 kakezan [5-24] 19

muscles 筋肉 kinniku [4-24] 17

museum 博物館 hakubutsukan [11-10] 30; [31-32] 71

mushroom きのこ kinoko [38-32] 85

music 音楽 ongaku [26-20] 61

musician 音楽家 ongakuka [25-8] 58

Myanmar ミャンマー Myanmā [32-3] 72

N

name 名前 namae [1-23] 11

nationality 国籍 kokuseki [1-27] 11

natural gas 天然ガス tennen-gasu [28-16] 65

near 近い chikai [8-25] 25; [13-42] 35

nearby そば soba [13-50] 35

neck 首 kubi [4-4] 16

necktie ネクタイ nekutai [10-15] 28

neighbor 隣人 rinjin [2-32] 12; [11-29] 31

nephew 甥 oi [2-23] 13

nervous system 神経系 shinkeikei [4-39] 17

network; Internet ネットワーク; インターネット nettowāku; intānetto [24-25] 56

network card ネットワークカード nettowāku kādo [23-34] 55

network security ネットワークセキュリティー nettowāku sekyuritii [23-39] 55

network ネットワーク nettowāku [23-23] 55

neurology 神経内科 shinkei-naika [27-32] 63

new 新しい atarashii [8-4] 24

New Year 新年 Shinnen [18-2] 44

newspaper 新聞 shinbun [19-9] 46

next; side 隣 tonari [13-49] 35

next month 来月 raigetsu [16-44] 41

next time 今度 kondo [15-29] 39

next week 来週 raishū [16-43] 41

next year 来年 rainen [16-33] 41

niece 姪 mei [2-25] 13

night 夜 yoru [15-16] 39

night stays 泊 haku; paku [22-21] 53

Nikon ニコン Nikon [24-20] 57

nine 九 kyū; ku [5-9] 18

Nintendo 任天堂 Nintendō [24-17] 57

no いいえ iie [8-18] 25

noon 正午 shōgo [15-23] 39

north 北 kita [13-6] 34

North America 北アメリカ Kita Amerika [32-14] 73

northeast 北東 hokutō [13-8] 34

northwest 北西 hokusei [13-7] 34

nose 鼻 hana [4-9] 16

not to have ない nai [8-16] 25

notebook ノート nōto [19-18] 47

November 十一月 jūichigatsu [16-28] 41

now 今 ima [15-17] 39

nuclear energy 原子 genshi-ryoku [28-17] 65

numbers 数; 番号 kazu; bangō [5-28] 19

nurse 看護師 kangoshi [27-3] 62

nursery school 幼稚園 yōchien [20-29] 49

nuts ナッツ nattsu [37-41] 83

O

oatmeal; rolled oats オートミール ōtomiiru [35-26] 79; [37-43] 83

oats オーツ麦 ōtsu mugi [37-34] 83

occurrences, times 回 kai [22-13] 53

occurrences, times, degrees 度 do [22-12] 53

ocean 海 umi [28-7] 64

Oceania オセアニア Oseania [32-19] 73

October 十月 jūgatsu [16-27] 41

octopus タコ tako [38-13] 84

odd numbers 奇数 kisū [5-27] 19

of course もちろん mochiron [28-37] 65

office 事務所; オフィス jimusho; ofisu [25-15] 58

office water dispenser ウォーターサーバー wōtā sābā [36-28] 81

oil 石油 sekiyu [28-22] 65

ointment 軟膏 nankō [27-37] 63

old 古い furui [8-4] 24; 年をとっています toshi o totte imasu [8-10] 25

older brother お兄さん oniisan [2-19] 13

older sister お姉さん onēsan [2-18] 13

olive oil オリーブ油 oriibu oiru [38-65] 86

oncology 腫瘍科 shuyōka [27-30] 63

one 一 ichi [5-1] 18

one half 半分; 二分の一 hanbun; nibun no ichi [5-11] 18

one quarter 四分の一 yonbun no ichi [5-13] 18

one side 片方 katahō [13-52] 35

one third 三分の一 sanbun no ichi [5-14] 18

one yen 一円 ichi en [9-9] 26

online オンライン onrain [23-32] 55

online friends ネット友達 netto tomodachi [24-2] 56

online shopping 通販 tsūhan [10-29] 29; オンラインショッピング onrain shoppingu [24-3] 56

operating system オペレーティングシステム; OS operētingu shisutemu; ōesu [23-20] 55

ophthalmology 眼科 ganka [27-28] 63

opportunity 機会 kikai [25-33] 59

opposite 向かい側 mukaigawa [13-44] 35

or (commonly used between sentences) それとも soretomo [34-31] 77

orange (color) オレンジ orenji [7-11] 22; (fruit) [37-3] 82

orange juice オレンジジュース orenji jūsu [36-4] 80

oregano オレガノ oregano [38-51] 85

organs 臓器 zōki [4-36] 17

other 他 hoka [10-37] 29

others 他人 tanin [31-46] 71

outside 外 soto [8-20] 25; 外側 sotogawa [13-33] 35

oven オーブン ōbun [3-27] 15

overcast 曇り kumori [14-6] 36

P

painting 絵画 kaiga [3-6] 14

palm oil パーム油; やし油 pāmuyu; yashiyu [38-86] 86

pancakes ホットケーキ hotto kēki [35-33] 79

panda パンダ panda [29-9] 66

papaya パパイヤ papaiya [37-10] 82

paper money 紙幣 shihei [9-2] 26

parents 両親 ryōshin [2-6] 12

park 公園 kōen [28-3] 64

parsley パセリ paseri [38-4] 84

part-time job アルバイト arubaito [25-29] 59

passenger 乗客 jōkyaku [12-19] 33

(in the) past 過去 kako [15-18] 39

passport パスポート pasupōto [31-8] 70

password パスワード pasuwādo [23-17] 55

pasta; spaghetti パスタ; スパゲッティ pasuta; supagetti [35-4] 78

patient 患者 kanja [27-5] 62

peach 桃 momo [37-9] 82

peach blossoms 桃の花 momo no hana [17-7] 42

peacock 孔雀 kujaku [29-18] 67

peanut oil ピーナッツオイル piinattsu oiru [38-84] 86

peanuts ピーナッツ piinattsu [37-20] 83

pear なし nashi [37-5] 82

pecans ピーカンナッツ piikan nattsu [37-22] 83

pedestrian 歩行者 hokōsha [11-34] 31

pediatrics 小児科 shōnika [27-26] 63

pen ペン pen [19-13] 47

pencil 鉛筆 enpitsu [19-20] 47

pencil sharpener 鉛筆削り enpitsu kezuri [19-16] 47

people counter 一人、二人、三人 ... hitori, futari, sannin ... [22-2] 52

people (honorific) 名 mei [22-16] 53

pepper こしょう koshō [38-74] 86

persimmon 柿 kaki [37-18] 82

pertaining to … に関する … ni kansuru [27-48] 63

Philippines フィリピン Firipin [32-5] 72

pharmacist 薬剤師 yakuzaishi [25-6] 58

phone cards テレホンカード terehon kādo [24-30] 56

phone charger 充電器 jūdenki [24-29] 56

photocopier コピー機 kopiiki [20-7] 48

photograph 写真 shashin [31-16] 70

photographer 写真家 shashinka [25-12] 59

phrase 文句 monku [21-17] 51

physical education 体育 taiiku [19-5] 46

physics 物理 butsuri [19-39] 47

physiotherapy 理学療法 rigaku ryōhō [27-31] 63

piano ピアノ piano [26-9] 60

pillow 枕 makura [3-19] 14

pills 錠剤 jōzai [27-16] 62

pilot パイロット pairotto [25-13] 59

pine nuts 松の実 matsu no mi [37-28] 83

pineapple パイナップル painappuru [37-8] 82

pink ピンク pinku [7-12] 22

pistachios ピスタチオ pisutachio [37-23] 83

pizza ピザ piza [35-3] 78

place 場所 basho [13-51] 35

plane ticket 航空券 kōkūken [31-19] 71

plant 植える ueru [28-19] 65

plate 皿 sara [34-11] 76

poem 詩; 歌 shi; uta [21-19] 51

police station 警察署 keisatsusho [11-17] 31

pollution 公害 kōgai [28-4] 64

pop group ポップグループ poppu gurūpu [26-15] 61

pop music ポップス poppusu [26-24] 61

pork 豚肉 buta niku [38-5] 84

ports ポート pōto [23-14] 54

Portuguese ポルトガル語 Porutogarugo [33-18] 75

position 職 shoku [25-35] 59

post office 郵便局 yūbinkyoku [11-16] 31

postcard 葉書 hagaki [31-30] 71

potato じゃがいも jagaimo [38-28] 85

potted plant 鉢植え hachiue [3-47] 15

prescription 処方箋 shohōsen [27-35] 63

price 値段 nedan [9-20] 27

principal 校長 kōchō [20-17] 49

private school 私立学校 shiritsu gakkō [20-27] 49

professor 教授 kyōju [20-12] 48

program 演目 enmoku [26-23] 61

public bus バス basu [12-12] 33

public school 公立学校 kōritsu gakkō [20-28] 49

pudding プリン purin [35-8] 78

pumpkin カボチャ kabocha [38-47] 85

pumpkin seeds カボチャの種 kabocha no tane [37-30] 83

punctual 時間を守る jikan o mamoru [15-26] 39

purple 紫 murasaki [7-8] 22

purpose 目的 mokuteki [19-51] 47

Q

quarter (hour) 十五分 jūgofun [15-7] 38

quiet 静か shizuka [28-10] 64

R

racket ラケット raketto [30-23] 69

radiology 放射線科 hōshasenka [27-33] 63

railing 手すり tesuri [3-3] 14

rain 雨 ame [14-10] 36

raincoat レインコート reinkōto [14-2] 36

raining 雨降り amefuri [14-11] 36

rainstorm 暴風雨 bōfūu [14-28] 37

ramen noodles ラーメン rāmen [34-18] 77

real 本物 honmono [8-27] 25

receipt 領収書; レシート ryōshūsho; reshiito [9-29] 27

receive 受ける ukeru [8-2] 24

recycling リサイクル risaikuruu [28-20] 65

red 赤 aka [7-2] 22

red wine 赤ワイン aka wain [36-19] 81

refrigerator 冷蔵庫 reizōko [3-26] 15

refund 払い戻し haraimodoshi [10-42] 29

relatives 親戚 shinseki [2-31] 12

compulsory 必修 hisshū [20-42] 49

respiratory system 呼吸器系 kokyūkikei [4-38] 17

restaurant レストラン resutoran [31-39] 71

rice 米 kome [37-38] 83

rice wine 料理酒 ryōrishu [38-77] 86

rice wine/sake 酒 sake [36-23] 81

right 正しい tadashii [8-26] 25

right side 右側 migigawa [13-27] 35

river 川 kawa [28-8] 64

road 道路 dōro [11-36] 31

roasted beef with dipping sauce 焼肉 yakiniku [34-22] 77

roasted chicken kebab 焼き鳥 yakitori [34-23] 77

roof 屋根 yane [3-53] 14

room 部屋 heya [3-22] 14

rosemary ローズマリー rōzumarii [38-7] 84

roses バラ bara [18-17] 45

rowing ボート競技 bōto kyōgi [30-18] 69

ruler 物差し; 定規 monosashi; jōgi [19-17] 47

rugby ラグビー ragubii [30-3] 68

running ランニング ranningu [30-9] 68

Russian ロシア語 Roshiago [33-3] 74

S

S size エスサイズ esu saizu [7-31] 23

sad 悲しい kanashii [8-31] 25

sage セージ sēji [38-52] 85

salad サラダ sarada [35-13] 78

salt 塩 shio [38-70] 86

sandwich サンドイッチ sandoitchi [35-2] 78

Santa Claus サンタクロース santakurōsu [18-24] 45

satisfied 満足 manzoku [1-9] 10

Saturday 土曜日 Doyōbi [16-17] 40

sausage ソーセージ sōsēji [35-16] 78

savings 貯金 chokin [9-16] 27

scallions; spring onions 青ねぎ aonegi [38-38] 85

scarf スカーフ sukāfu [10-20] 29

school 学校 gakkō [20-16] 49

science 科学 kagaku [19-35] 47; [20-11] 48

scissors ハサミ hasami [19-21] 47

screen 画面 gamen [23-2] 54

seafood 魚介類 gyokairui [38-11] 84

seasonings 調味料 chōmiryō [38-61] 86

seasonings sprinkled on rice ふりかけ furikake [38-72] 86

second(s) 秒 byō [15-3] 38; [22-17] 53

secretary 秘書 hisho [25-17] 58

self 自分 jibun [2-36] 12

selfie セルフィー; 自撮り serufii; jidori [24-14] 57

senior high school 高校 kōkō [20-33] 49

senior year in college 大学四年生 daigaku yonensei [20-38] 49

sentence 文章 bunshō [21-16] 51

September 九月 kugatsu [16-26] 41

sesame oil ゴマ油 goma abura [38-64] 86

sesame seeds ゴマ goma [37-33] 83

set menu 定食 teishoku [34-1] 76

seven 七 nana; shichi [5-7] 18

Seven continents of the world 世界の七大陸 Sekai no nanatairiku [32-13] 73

seven spice 七味 shichimi [38-71] 86

several times 何度か nando ka [27-43] 63

shape 形 katachi [7-38] 23

sheep 羊 hitsuji [29-12] 67

Shinto shrine 神社 shingō [11-37] 31

ship; boat 客船 kyakusen [12-14] 33

shirt シャツ shatsu [10-14] 28

shoes 靴 kutsu [10-13] 28

shop 店 mise [10-22] 29; [11-3] 30

shop staff 店員 ten'in [10-25] 29

shopping bag レジ袋; エコバッグ reji bukuro; eko baggu [10-4] 28

shopping center; mall ショッピングモール shoppingu mōru [11-22] 31

short 背が低い se ga hikui [8-5] 24; 短い mijikai [8-9] 24

short essay 作文 sakubun [21-18] 51

shoulder 肩 kata [4-23] 17

shower シャワー shawā [3-41] 15

shrimp; prawns エビ ebi [38-15] 84

SIM card SIMカード shimu kādo [24-35] 56

sidewalk 歩道 hodō [11-28] 31

sightseeing 観光 kankō [31-28] 71

silver 銀色 gin'iro [7-14] 22

similar; alike 似ている nite iru [29-37] 67

simple 簡単 kantan [21-29] 51

Singapore シンガポール Shingapōru [32-10] 72

singer 歌手 kashu [26-29] 61

sink 洗面台 senmendai [3-40] 15

sister-in-law 義理の姉妹 giri no shimai [2-34] 12

sisters 姉妹 shimai [2-16] 13

six 六 roku [5-6] 18

size 大きさ; サイズ ōkisa; saizu [7-39] 23

skeletal system 骨格 kokkaku [4-40] 17

skiing スキー sukii [30-17] 69

skin 皮膚 hifu [4-41] 17

skirt スカート sukāto [10-8] 28

skyscraper 超高層ビル chōkōsō biru [11-12] 30

sliced raw fish 刺身 sashimi [34-19] 77

slow 遅い osoi [8-28] 25

slow down もっとゆっくり motto yukkuri [12-26] 33

small 小さい chiisai [7-37] 23; [8-11] 25

small animals 一匹、二匹、三匹 … ippiki, nihiki, sanbiki … [22-7] 52

small or round objects 一個、二個、三個 … ikko, niko, sanko … [22-9] 52

small change 小銭 kozeni [9-14] 27

large animals 一頭、二頭、三頭 … i-tō, ni-tō, san-tō … [22-8] 52

smaller もっと小さい motto chiisai [7-41] 23

smartphone スマホ; スマートフォン sumaho; sumātofon [24-1] 56

smartwatch スマートウォッチ sumātowotchi [15-14] 39

snake 蛇 hebi [29-17] 67

snow 雪 yuki [14-15] 36

snowball fights 雪合戦 ukigassen [17-15] 43

soccer サッカー sakkā [30-2] 68

sociology 社会学 shakaigaku [19-36] 47

socks 靴下 kutsushita [10-12] 28

soda ソーダ sōda [36-27] 81

sofa ソファ sofa [3-15] 14

software ソフト（ウェア） sofuto (wea) [23-19] 55

solar energy 太陽エネルギー taiyō enerugii [28-9] 64

son 息子 musuko [2-1] 12

son-in-law 義理の息 musume-muko; giri no musuko [2-28] 12

Sony ソニー Sonii [24-16] 57

soon; very soon もうすぐ mōsugu [13-57] 35

soup スープ sūpu [34-25] 77

south 南 minami [13-13] 34

South America 南アメリカ Minami Amerika [32-15] 73

southeast 南東 nantō [13-12] 34

southwest 南西 nansei [13-11] 34

souvenir shop 土産物店 miyagemonoten [31-14] 70

soy sauce 醤油 shōyu [38-62] 86

soy milk 豆乳 tōnyū [36-9] 80

soybean 大豆 daizu [38-69] 86

soybean paste 味噌 miso [38-68] 86

Spanish スペイン語 Supeingo [33-6] 74

special 特別 tokubetsu [34-29] 77

spinach ほうれん草 hōrensō [38-21] 84

spoon スプーン supūn [34-14] 76

sports car スポーツカー supōtsuka [12-10] 32

sports day event 運動会 undōkai [18-9] 44

sports drinks スポーツドリンク supōtsu dorinku [36-17] 80

sports shirt; sweatshirt トレーナー torēnā [30-25] 69

sports shoes; sneakers スニーカー suniikā [30-26] 69

spring 春 haru [17-1] 42

sprint 短距離走 tankyorisō [30-8] 68

stadium スタジアム sutajiamu [11-15] 31

staff; personnel; employee 職員; 社員 shokuin; shain [25-26] 59

Star Festival 七夕 Tanabata [18-7] 44

starch でん粉; 片栗粉 denpun; katakuriko [38-80] 86

steak ステーキ sutēki [35-15] 78

sticky rice cake お餅 omochi [18-11] 44

(stomach) is full お腹がいっぱいです onaka ga ippai [8-22] 25

strange 不思議 fushigi [29-41] 67

strawberry いちご ichigo [37-15] 82

street 道 michi [11-4] 30

street corner 街角 machikado [11-30] 31

stroke order 書き順 kakijun [21-11] 51

stomach 胃 i [4-49] 17

strong signal 電波が強い denpa ga tsuyoi [24-12] 57

stopwatch ストップウォッチ sutoppuwotchi [15-13] 39

story 物語 monogatari [19-31] 47

stove ストーブ sutōbu [3-31] 15

student 生徒; 学生 seito; gakusei [20-14] 48

study room 勉強部屋 benkyō-beya [3-32] 15

study time 勉強時間 **benkyō jikan** [6-35] *20*

suburb 郊外 **kōgai** [11-25] *31*

subtraction 引き算 **hikizan** [5-23] *19*

subway 地下鉄 **chikatetsu** [12-11] *33*

suddenly 突然 **totsuzen** [15-35] *39*

sugar 砂糖 **satō** [38-75] *86*

suitcase スーツケース **xsūtsukēsu** [31-5] *70*

summer 夏 **natsu** [17-2] *42*

summer vacation 夏休み **natsuyasumi** [18-27] *45*

sun 太陽 **taiyō** [14-26] *37*

sunblock lotion 日焼け止め **hiyakedome** [17-16] *43*

Sunday 日曜日 **Nichiyōbi** *40*

sunflower seeds ヒマワリの種 **himawari no tane** [37-32] *83*

sunny side up eggs 卵焼き；目玉焼き **tamagoyaki; medamayaki** [35-21] *79*

sunny weather 晴れた天気 **hareta tenki** [14-36] *37*

sunshade; parasole 日傘 **higasa** [17-10] *42*

supermarket スーパー **sūpā** [11-5] *30*

surname 苗字 **myōji** [1-24] *11*

sushi 寿司 **sushi** [34-20] *77*

sweater セーター **sētā** [14-19] *37*

swimming 水泳 **suiei** [30-19] *69*

T

table テーブル **tēburu** [3-14] *14*

table lamp 電気スタンド **denki sutando** [3-33] *15*

table tennis 卓球 **takkyū** [30-1] *68*

tablet タブレット **taburetto** [23-3] *54*

Tagalog タガログ語 **Tagarogugo** [33-17] *75*

talent; ability 才能 **sainō** [19-45] *47*

tall 背が高い **se ga takai** [8-5] *24*

tap water 水道水 **suidōsui** [36-11] *80*

tarragon タラゴン **taragon** [38-54] *85*

tasty; delicious 美味しい **oishii** [35-30] *79*

tax 税金 **zeikin** [9-31] *27*

tax free 免税 **menzei** [10-41] *29*

taxi タクシー **takushii** [12-2] *32*

tea お茶 **ocha** [36-7] *80*

teacher 先生 **sensei** [20-6] *48*; 教師 **kyōshi** [20-18] *49*

teeth 歯 **ha** [4-12] *16*

telephone number 電話番号 **denwa bangō** [24-24] *58*

telephone operator オペレーター **operētā** [25-10] *58*

television テレビ **terebi** [3-10] *14*

temple 寺 **tera** [11-35] *31*

tempura 天ぷら **tenpura** [34-21] *77*

ten 十 **jū** [5-10] *18*

ten yen 十円 **jū en** [9-6] *26*

tennis テニス **tenisu** [30-22] *69*

test テスト **tesuto** [19-44] *47*

textbook 教科書 **kyōkasho** [20-26] *49*

texting ショートメッセージ **shōto messēji** [24-27] *56*

Thai タイ語 **Taigo** [33-15] *75*

Thailand タイ **Tai** [32-2] *72*

Thanksgiving 感謝祭（勤労感謝の日）**Kanshasai (Kinrō kansha no hi)** [18-18] *45*

that それ **sore** [29-35] *67*

the east 東部 **tōbu** [13-45] *35*

the news ニュース **nyūsu** [19-8] *46*

the north 北部 **hokubu** [13-48] *35*

the same as 同じ **onaji** [10-31] *29*

the south 南部 **nanbu** [13-46] *35*

the west 西部 **seibu** [13-47] *35*

the year after next 再来年 **sarainen** [16-34] *41*

the year before last 一昨年 **ototoshi** [16-31] *41*

there; over there そこ；あそこ **soko; asoko** [13-3] *34*

thesis; dissertation 論文 **ronbun** [21-20] *51*

thick wheat noodles うどん **udon** [34-16] *77*

thigh 腿 **momo** [4-27] *17*

thin 痩せています **yasete imasu** [8-13] *25*

thin, flat object counter: like paper, shirts, and tickets 一枚、二枚、三枚 … **ichimai, nimai, sanmai …** [22-3] *52*

things もの **mono** [10-39] *29*

thirsty 喉が渇いている **nodo ga kawaite iru** [36-14] *80*

this year 今年 **kotoshi** [16-32] *41*

three 三 **san** [5-3] *18*

three quarters 四分の三 **yonbun no san** [5-12] *18*

thunder 雷 **kaminari** [14-13] *36*

thunderstorm 嵐 **larashi** [14-14] *36*

Thursday 木曜日 **Mokuyōbi** [16-15] *40*

thyme タイム **taimu** [38-53] *85*

ticket counter 切符売り場 **kippu uriba** [12-31] *33*

tiger トラ **tora** [29-4] *66*

time 時間 **jikan** [15-20] *39*

tired; worn out 疲れている **tsukarete iru** [14-61] *63*

to accomplish 完成する **kansei suru** [28-34] *65*

to add 足す **tasu** [5-20] *19*

to affect 影響する **eikyō suru** [28-35] *65*

to agree 賛成する **sansei suru** [6-43] *20*

to allow; to cause させる **saseru** [13-58] *35*

to answer 答える **kotaeru** [6-22] *20*; [19-6] *46*

to appear 現れる **arawareru** [29-39] *67*

to appreciate; to enjoy 楽しむ **tanoshimu** [26-19] *61*

to arrive 着く **tsuku** [8-19] *25*

to ask 質問する **shitsumon suru** [6-19] *20*

to ask directions 道をたずねる **michi o tazuneru** [13-16] *34*

to attend school 学校へ行く **gakkō e iku** [20-30] *49*

to bathe 入浴する **nyūyoku suru** [3-48] *15*

to be allergic; allergy アレルギー **arerugii** [37-48] *83*

to be concerned about 心配する **shinpai suru** [27-47] *63*

to be lost 道に迷う **michi ni mayou** [13-35] *35*

to be willing (to do something) 喜んで **yorokonde** [6-42] *20*

to become aware of 気づく **kizuku** [31-44] *71*

to begin 始まる **hajimaru** [8-24] *25*

to believe 信じる **shinjiru** [2-40] *12*

to borrow 借りる **kariru** [8-30] *25*

to bow お辞儀をする **ojigi o suru** [1-33] *11*

to breathe 呼吸する **kokyū suru** [6-21] *20*

to bring 持って来る **mottekuru** [10-38] *29*

to brush teeth 歯を磨く **ha o migaku** [6-11] *21*

to buy 買う **kau** [10-1] *28*

to call; to be called 呼ぶ **yobu** [1-12] *10*

to call a taxi タクシーを呼ぶ **takushii o yobu** [12-34] *33*

to catch a bus バスに乗る **basu ni noru** [12-20] *33*

to catch a cold 風邪をひく **kaze o hiku** [27-10] *62*

to catch sight of 見える **mieru** [6-23] *20*

to chat online チャットする **chatto suru** [23-38] *55*

to clean 掃除する **sōji suru** [3-44] *15*

to click クリックする **kurikku suru** [23-29] *55*

to close 閉める **shimeru** [8-12] *25*

to come 来る **kuru** [8-17] *25*

to come across 出会う **deau** [31-42] *71*

to compare prices 値段を比べる **nedan o kuraberu** [10-28] *29*

to congratulate; to celebrate 祝う **iwau** [1-13] *10*

to consider 考える **kangaeru** [13-61] *35*

to cook; to prepare a meal 料理する **ryōri suru** [6-27] *20*

to cough 咳が出る **seki ga deru** [27-11] *62*

to cry 泣く **naku** [6-3] *20*

to cycle 自転車に乗る **jitensha ni noru** [30-12] *68*

to dance 踊る；ダンスする **odoru; dansu suru** [26-6] *60*

to dare 敢えて **aete** [29-40] *67*

to discover 見つける **mitsukeru** [27-45] *63*

to divide 割る **waru** [5-17] *19*

to do household chores 家事をする **kaji o suru** [6-36] *20*

to download ダウンロードする **daunrōdo suru** [23-30] *55*

to draw blood 採血 **saiketsu** [27-6] *62*

to drill 訓練する **kunren suru** [21-33] *51*

to drink 飲む **nomu** [36-13] *80*

to drive a car 車を運転する **kuruma o unten suru** [12-24] *33*

to drizzle 小雨 **kosame** [17-9] *42*

to end 終わる **owaru** [8-24] *25*

to exceed 優れる **sugureru** [20-44] *49*

to exercise; sports 運動する **undō suru** [30-6] *68*

to express 表現する **hyōgen suru** [26-32] *61*

to fall sick 病気になる **byōki ni naru** [27-13] *62*

to feel 感じがする **kanji ga suru** [27-42] *62*

to feel anxious 心配する **shinpai suru** [13-63] *35*

to feel reassured 安心する **anshin suru** [27-46] *63*

to find 探す；見つける **sagasu; mitsukeru** [31-40] *71*

to flower 咲く **saku** [17-8] *42*

to forget 忘れ **wasureru** [8-23] *25*

to get angry 怒る **okoru; ikaru** [6-39] *20*

to give directions 道を教える **michi o oshieru** [13-21] *34*

to go 行く **iku** [8-17] *25*

to go to work; to get off work 仕事へ行く；仕事から帰る **shigoto e iku; shigoto kara kaeru** [6-26] *20*

to graduate 卒業する **sotsugyō suru** [20-45] *49*

to greet 挨拶をする **aisatsu o suru** [1-34] *11*

to go straight まっすぐ行ってください **massugu itte kudasai** [12-29] *33*; 直進 **chokushin** [13-31] *35*

to go through 通る **tōru** [13-54] *35*

to go to school 学校へ行く **gakkō e iku** [6-24] *20*

to go to work 出勤する **shukkin suru** [25-23] *59*

to have ある **aru** [8-16] *25*

to have breakfast 朝ご飯を食べ **asagohan o taberu** [6-31] *20*

to have dinner 晩ご飯を食べる **bangohan o taberu** [6-33] *20*

to have lunch 昼ご飯を食べる **hirugohan o taberu** [6-32] *20*

to help 手伝う **tetsudau** [6-16] *21*; 助ける **tasukeru** [13-62] *35*

to hug 抱きあう **dakiau** [1-29] *11*

to improve 上手になる **jōzu ni naru** [19-48] *47*

to inspect 調べる **shiraberu** [25-22] *59*

to introduce 紹介する **shōkai suru** [1-7] *10*

to kiss キスする；接吻する **kisu suru; seppun suru** [1-30] *11*

to know 知る **shiru** [1-26] *11*

to laugh 笑う **warau** [6-4] *20*

to learn; to study 勉強する **benkyō suru** [19-3] *46*

to leave 出かける **dekakeru** [8-19] *25*; [13-55] *35*

to lend 貸す **kasu** [8-30] *25*

to listen 聞く **kiku** [6-13] *20*

to look; see 見る **miru** [6-2] *20*

to look like; to resemble に見える **ni mieru** [29-38] *67*

to love 大好き **daisuki** [19-33] *47*

to major 専攻する senkō suru [20-40] 49

to make a phone call 電話をかける denwa o kakeru [24-10] 56

to make a snowman 雪だるまを作る yukidaruma o tsukuru [17-12] 43

to make a small talk おしゃべりする oshaberi suru [1-36] 11

to meet 会う au [1-3] 10

to move 引っ越す hikkosu [6-15] 21

to multiply 掛ける kakeru [5-18] 19

to open 開ける akeru [8-12] 25

to order 注文する chūmon suru [34-27] 77

to pay attention to 注意する chūi suru [31-43] 71

to perform 上演する jōen suru [26-22] 61

to perform (on a musical instrument) 演奏する ensō suru [26-27] 61

to photocopy コピーをとる kopii o toru [20-8] 48

to play 遊ぶ asobu [6-20] 20

to play a string instrument 弾く hiku [26-25] 61

to prepare 準備する junbi suru [21-35] 51

to practice 練習する renshū suru [19-24] 47

to put on 着る kiru [8-14] 25

to raise your hand 手をあげる te o ageru [20-9] 48

to read 読む yomu [19-2] 46

to receive a phone call 電話を受ける denwa o ukeru [24-11] 56

to relax くつろぐ kutsurogu [6-30] 20

to request 要求する yōkyū suru [6-41] 20

to remember 覚える oboeru [8-23] 25

to resolve 解決する kaiketsu suru [6-40] 20

to review 復習する fukushū suru [19-25] 47

to ride a bike 自転車に乗る jitensha ni noru [12-25] 33

to ride a train 電車に乗る densha ni noru [12-22] 33

to roast; to bake 焼く yaku [35-32] 79

to scan スキャンする sukyan suru [23-11] 54

to search online 検索する kensaku suru [23-41] 55

to send an email 電子メールを送る denshi mēru o okuru [23-40] 55

to sell 売る uru [10-2] 28

to sign in ログイン roguin [23-16] 55

to sing 歌を歌う uta o utau [26-12] 61

to sit 座る suwaru [6-6] 20

to shake hands 握手する akushu suru [1-28] 11

to shop 買い物をする kaimono o suru [10-3] 28

to sleep 寝る neru [6-7] 21

to smile 笑う warau [1-31] 11

to snow 雪が降る yuki ga furu [14-16] 36

to speak 伝える tsutaeru [6-13] 21

to stand 立つ tatsu [6-5] 20

to start a conversation 話しかける hanashi-kakeru [1-35] 11

to strive 一生懸命 isshōkenmei [21-34] 51

to subtract 引く hiku [5-19] 19

to take 取る toru [31-41] 71

to take a shower シャワーを浴びる shawā o abiru [6-28] 20

to take medicine 薬を飲む kusuri o nomu [27-14] 62

to take off 脱ぐ nugu [8-14] 25

to talk 話す hanasu [1-37] 11; [6-12] 21

to teach 教える oshieru [20-5] 48

to tell 教える oshieru [13-53] 35

to think 思う omou [13-60] 35

to turn left 左へ曲がる hidari e magaru [13-30] 35

to turn right 右へ曲がる migi e magaru [13-30] 35

to understand わかる wakaru [19-23] 47; 理解する rikai suru [21-30] 51

to use the internet インターネットを使う intānetto o tsukau [23-31] 55

to wake up 起きる okiru [6-10] 21

to walk the dog 犬を散歩させる inu o sanpo saseru [6-17] 21

to wash my hair 髪を洗う kami o arau [6-29] 20

to watch TV テレビを見る terebi o miru [6-8] 21

to wave 手を振る te o furu [1-32] 11

to withdraw money 引き出す hikidasu [9-18] 27

to work overtime 残業する zangyō suru [25-30] 59

to write 書く kaku [6-9] 21

toast トースト tōsuto [35-22] 79

toaster トースター tōsutā [3-30] 15

today 今日 kyō [16-8] 40

toes 足指 ashiyubi [4-16] 16

tofu 豆腐 tōfu [38-42] 85

toilet bowl 便器 benki [3-43] 15

tomato トマト tomato [38-26] 85

tomorrow 明日 ashita; asu [16-9] 40

tongue 舌 shita [4-11] 16

top rank 上位 jōi [19-49] 47

topic 題 dai [20-41] 49

tour guide ガイド gaido [31-6] 70

tourist attraction 観光地 kankōchi [31-7] 70

tourist information center 観光案内所 kankō annaisho [31-29] 71

toys おもちゃ omocha [10-18] 29

traffic 交通 kōtsū [11-33] 31

traffic lights 信号 shingō [11-37] 31

train 電車 densha [12-15] 33

train schedule 電車時刻表 densha jikokuhyō [12-30] 33

train station 駅 eki [11-9] 30; [31-35] 71

tram 路面電車 romen densha [12-17] 33

translation 翻訳 hon'yaku [21-23] 51

travel agency 旅行会社 ryokō gaisha [31-24] 71

travel by airplane 飛行機で旅行する hikōki de ryokō suru [31-10] 70

travel by bus 観光バスで旅行する kankōbasu de ryokō suru [31-12] 70

travel by rail 電車で旅行する densha de ryokō suru [31-11] 70

travel guidebook 旅行ガイドブック ryokō gaidobukku [31-23] 71

traveler 旅行者 ryokōsha [31-3] 70

tree 木 ki [28-15] 65

trousers ズボン zubon [10-10] 28

truck トラック torakku [12-5] 32

trumpet トランペット toranpetto [26-8] 60

turkey 七面鳥 shichimenchō [35-10] 78

Tuesday 火曜日 Kayōbi [16-13] 40

Turkish トルコ語 Torukogo [33-7] 74

turn left/turn right 左/右に曲がってください hidari/migi ni magatte kudasai [12-28] 33

Twitter ツイッター Tsuittā [24-5] 56

two 二 ni [5-2] 18

two thirds 三分の二 sanbun no ni [5-15] 18

types of meat 肉の種類 niku no shurui [38-57] 85

typhoon 台風 taifū [14-17] 36

U

Uber ウーバー ūbā [12-35] 33

umbrella 傘 kasa [14-1] 36

uncle おじさん ojisan [2-11] 13

university; college 大学 daigaku [20-34] 49

up 上 ue [8-1] 24

USB flash drive ユーエスビーフラッシュドライブ yūesubii furasshu doraibu [23-13] 54

V

vacation 休み yasumi [31-18] 71

vaccination 予防接種 yobō sesshu [31-25] 71

Valentine's Day バレンタインデー Barentain dē [18-15] 45

vegetables 野菜 yasai [38-17] 84

vegetarian 菜食 ssaishoku [34-26] 77

vein 静脈 jōmyaku [4-46] 17

very; extremely とても totemo [29-36] 67; 非常に hijō ni [23-48] 55

vessels 血管 kekkan [4-43] 17

video 動画 dōga [24-34] 56

video game テレビゲーム terebi gēmu [23-8] 54

Vietnam ベトナム Betonamu [32-4] 72

Vietnamese ベトナム語 Betonamugo [33-12] 75

vinegar 酢 su [38-66] 86

violin バイオリン baiorin [26-4] 60

virus ウィルス wirusu [23-21] 55

visa ビザ biza [31-22] 71

vocabulary 語彙 goi [21-13] 51

vocabulary cards 単語カード tango kādo [21-4] 50

volleyball バレーボール barēbōru [30-20] 69

W

waiter; waitress ウェイター；ウェイトレス weita; weitoresu [25-31] 59; [34-2] 76

waiting room 待合室 machiaishitsu [27-19] 63

walking 歩く aruku [30-21] 69

wall 壁 kabe [3-9] 14

walnuts くるみ kurumi [37-21] 83

warm 暖かい atatakai [17-5] 42

wasabi わさび wasabi [38-73] 86

washroom お手洗い；トイレ otearai; toire [3-38] 15

water 水 mizu [28-26] 65; [36-12] 80

water play 水遊び mizuasobi [17-11] 42

water tap 蛇口 jaguchi [3-39] 15

watermelon スイカ suika [37-19] 82

watermelon seeds スイカの種 suika no tane [37-31] 83

weak signal 電波が弱い（悪い） denpa ga yowai (warui) [24-13] 57

Wednesday 水曜日 Suiyōbi [16-14] 40

week 週間 shūkan [16-35] 41

weekday 平日 heijitsu [6-37] 20

weekend 週末 shūmatsu [6-38] 20

weather 天気 tenki [14-32] 37

weather forecast 天気予報 tenki yohō [14-33] 37

web address; URL ウェブアドレス webua doresu [23-26] 55

web design ウェブデザイン webu dezain [23-25] 55

web page ウェブページ webu pēji [23-24] 55

website ウェブサイト webusaito [23-18] 55

wefie; groufie グルーフィー gurūfii [24-15] 57

west 西 nishi [13-9] 34

Western breakfast 洋風の朝食 Yōfū no chōshoku [35-17] 79

Western-style food 洋食 Yōshoku [35-29] 79

What? 何ですか？ Nan desu ka? [1-8] 10

wheat 小麦 komugi [37-39] 83

where? どこ doko [13-1] 34

white 白 shiro [7-3] 22

whisky ウィスキー wisukii [36-21] 81

white 白 shiro [7-3] 22

White Day ホワイトデー howaitodē [18-32] 45

white rice 白いご飯 shiroi gohan [34-10] 76

white wine 白ワイン shiro wain [36-20] 81

whiteboard ホワイトボード howaitobōdo [20-1] 48

whole year; anniversary 周年 shūnen [18-30] 45

Why? どうして?; なぜ?
  Dōshite?; Naze? [1-39] *11*
wife 妻 **tsuma** [2-26] *12*
wifi WiFi **waifai** [23-42] *55*
wind 風 **kaze** [14-8] *36*
wind power 風力 **fūryoku** [28-12] *64*
window 窓 **mado** [3-18] *14*
windy 風が強い **kaze ga tsuyoi** [14-9] *36*
winter 冬 **fuyu** [17-4] *42*
winter melon 冬瓜 **tōgan** [38-39] *85*
winter vacation 冬休み **fuyuyasumi** [18-28] *45*
wolf オオカミ **ōkami** [29-16] *67*

word(s) 単語 **tango** [19-30] *47*; [21-10] *51*
work 仕事 **shigoto** [25-25] *59*
workbook ワークブック **wākubukku** [20-26] *49*
world 世界 **sekai** [32-29] *73*
wound; cut 傷口 **kizuguchi** [27-38] *63*
wrist watch 腕時計 **ude dokei** [10-5] *28*; [15-15] *39*
wrong 違う **chigau** [8-26] *25*

X
XL size エックスエルサイズ **ekkusu-eru saizu** [7-33] *23*

XS size エックスエスサイズ **ekkusu-esu saizu** [7-30] *23*

Y
year(s) 年 **nen; toshi** [16-4] *40*; **nen** [22-23] *53*
years (of age) 歳 **sai; toshi** [16-36] *41*
yellow 黄色 **kiiro** [7-5] *22*
yen; Japanese currency 円 **en** [9-1] *26*
yes 是 **hai** [8-18] *25*
yesterday 昨日 **kinō** [16-7] *40*
yogurt ヨーグルト **yōguruto** [35-35] *79*

you (polite) 貴方 **anata** [1-25] *11*
young 年下の **toshishita no** [2-37] *12*; 若い **wakai** [8-10] *25*
younger brother 弟 **otōto** [2-21] *13*
younger sister 妹 **imōto** [2-22] *13*
youth hostel ユースホステル **yūsu hosuteru** [31-26] *71*

Z
zebra シマウマ **bān mǎ** [29-2] *66*
zoo 動物園 **shimauma** [29-1] *66*
zucchini ズッキーニ **zukkiini** [38-49] *85*

Credits

JAPANESE AND ENGLISH VOICE RECORDERS: Keiko Skinner (Japanese) and JJ Skinner (English)

PHOTOS: **123rf.com:** Nopasorn Kowathanakul 44; Patrick Wallace 60, *back cover* / **Dreamstime.com:** Andreas Altenburger 44; Ciolca 50, *back cover*; Georgerudy 62; Li Lin 37; Natalya Aksenova 67 / **Shuttlestock.com:** 06photo 76; 89studio 47; 9dream studio *endpaper*; abc1234 77; adistock 52; Africa Studio 24, 29, 39, 48, 60, 80, 84; akepong srichaichana 83; Aleksandar Todorovic 73; AlenKadr 76; Alex Staroselsev 67; Alexander Raths 74; ALEXEY FILATOV 54; AlexLMX 46; Algol 66; Alhovik 23; Alice K 44; AlinaMD 37; All kind of people 41; all_about_people 13; amasterphotographer 82; AmyLv 83; anat chant 84; Anatolii Riepin 78; Andrey Burmakin 70; Andrey_Popov 21, 58; angelo lano 42; Annette Shaff 16; Anton_Ivanov 31; antpkr 24; Anucha Naisuntorn 38; ANUCHA PONGPATIMETH 26; anueing 18; aphotostory 64; Apple's Eyes Studio 62; arek_malang 21; Artem_Graf 81; artemisphoto 45; ArtFamily 35; ArtOfPhotos 44; ARZTSAMUI 26; Ase 64; asiandelight 43; Asier Romero 10, 13, 20; slysun 15, 16, 20, 21, 50, 62; Athapet Piruksa 54; Atstock Productions 63; AVAVA 58; AVprophoto *cover*; Ayakovlev 60; azure1 83; BalancePhoto 28; BaLL LunLa 62; Barone Firenze 57; Basico 77; beeboys 30, 50, *endpaper*; beibaoke 31; Belka10 80; bergamont 85; Beto Chagas 69; Billion Photos 50; Binh Thanh Bui 84; binik 52; Bjoern Wylezich 57; Bloomicon 54; BlueSkyImage 69; Bo1982 77; Bohbeh 46, 76; bonchan 76, 81; BOONCHUAY PROMJIAM 67; bright 24; Butterfly Hunter 16; By natu 77; Bychykhin Olexandr 44; Byjeng 31, *endpaper*; byvalet 73; Caftor 23; Captblack76 60, *endpaper*; Catwalk Photos 75; CHAjAMP 20, 39; Chalermchai Chamnanyon 83; chanut iamnoy 25; charnsitr 39; Chinaview 80; Chones 80; Christian Jung 82; Chuanthit Kunlayanamitre 82, 84; Chubarov Alexandr 22; Chutima Chaochaiya 48; chuyuss *endpaper*; Cineberg 57; Clari Massimiliano 77, *endpaper*; Coffeemill 44; Constantine Pankin 44; Coprid 43, *endpaper*; cowardlion 30, 33; Creativa Images 12, 21; Csdesign86 38; Dacian G 54; dailin 79; Dario Sabljak 60; Dark Moon Pictures 36; Dashu Xinganling 64; David Gilder 14; Dean Drobot 71, 77; defpicture 66; demidoff 37; Denis Rozhnovsky 54; DenisNata 15; Det-anan 14; Deyan Denchev 72; Dimasik_sh 15; diogoppr 78; Dmitriy Bryndin 74; dotshock 19, 52, 69; Dragan Milovanovic 28; Dragon Images 21, 46, 58, 59, 62, 68; dugdax 65; dwphotos 68; East 20; Eastfenceimage 13; Ebtikar 34; Egor Rodynchenko 82; Ekkamai Chaikanta 80; Elena Elisseeva 80; Elena Schweitzer 82; Elena Vasilchenko 62; Elina-Lava 75; Ellen C 50; Elnur 24, 28, 74; elwynn 17, 20, 28; Enlightened Media 83; Eric Isselee 25, 66, 67; ESB Professional 23, 35, 37, 48; Eugene Onischenko 68; Evan Lorne 57; Evangelos 32; Evgenyi 85; Farosofa 44; Fat Jackey 26; fear1ess 57; FeellFree 82; feelplus 35; Ferenc Szelepcsenyi 61; fizkes 64; Flashon Studio 58; Food1.it 78; fotohunter 42; Fototaras 42; Francesco83 18; Frank Fiedler 22; Freedom_Studio 35; furtseff 60; George Dolgikh 22, 78, 81; GMEVIPHOTO 79; Gnilenkov Aleksey 37; gnoparus 81; gogoiso 28; gontabunta 77; Goodmorning3am 66; GooDween123 36; gowithstock 80; Green Jo 42; gresei 79; Grobler du Preez 67; Gumpanat 27; Guzel Studio 73; Halfbottle 34; Hallgerd 36; HamsterMan 52; Hans Kim 34, 54; HelloRF Zcool 48; hijodepongol *cover, endpaper*; HomeStudio 24; Hong Vo 83; Howard Sandler 75; humphery 57; Hung Chung Chih 73; Hurst Photo 69; hxdbzxy 48; hxdyl 76; I'm friday 32; Iakov Filimonov 27, 34; iamlukyeee 44; iaodesign 78; IB Photography 54; icosha 31; ifong 24, 32; Igor Plotnikov 72; Igor Sh 80; Igors Rusakovs 85; iko 16; imtmphoto 11, 13; In Green 77; inbevel 43; IndigoLT 74; Inna Astakhova 67; iofoto 12; irin-k 29, 67; Ivan Demyanov 24; Ivan Smuk 69; Jane0606 57; jaroslava V 66; jazz3311 11, 81; JBOY 45; Jeanne McRight 59; jianbing Lee 46; JIANG HONGYAN 84, 85; jiangdi 85; Jiri Hera 86; John Bill 43; Jordi Muray 52; JPL Designs 60; kai keisuke 44; Kamenetskiy Konstantin 11, 68; kariphoto 84; Karkas 34; Karramba Production 69; Kate Aedon 21; Kaveex 64; kazoka 43, 77; Kazuki Nakagawa 36; kedrov 28; Keith Homan 80; kellyreekolibry 85; Ken Wolter 57; Kenishirotie 86; Khomulo Anna 70; Kim JinKwon 75; KingTa 31; Kirill Vorobyev 67; Kiselev Andrey Valerevich *cover*; KITSANANAN 83; Kletr 67; Kobby Dagan 61; Kokhanchikov 78; Kongsak 76; Kongsak *back cover*; Konstantin Zubarev 28-29; kowit1982 *endpaper*; KPG Ivary 39; KPG Payless2 33, 76; KPG_Payless 36; Ksander 54; kudla 70; Kzenon 25, 31, 45; Laaonnoi *spine, endpaper*; LazyFocus 66; leolintang 75; Leonid Ikan 42; leungchopan 10, 13, 57, 58, 59, 70; Lev Kropotov 65; LifetimeStock 74; Lim Yong Hian 82; Linda Bucklin 66; livingpitty 39; Ljupco Smokovski 65; Lonely 36; Lotus Images 45, 85; Louis W 26; LuckyImages 59; Lunghammer 68; M. Unal Ozmen 78; M.Stasy 46; Macrovector 15; Madlen 83; MAHATHIR MOHD YASIN 44; Makistock 59; Maks Narodenko 82, 83; Marcos Mesa Sam Wordley 23; margouillat photo 78; Maridav 42, 69; Mariusz Szczygiel 80; maroke 10, 59; martinho Smart 14; Matej Kastelic 70; mathom 24; Maxim Tupikov 69; maximmmmum 83; Maxx-Studio 70; Mega Pixel 27; michaeljung 70, 74; MidoSemsem 82; Milles Studio 45; minianne 26; Ministr-84 32; mirana 55; miya227 10, 27; Monkey Business Images 12, 13, 14, 21, 46, 58; monticello 78, 79; mountainpix 75; MP_P 39; mphot 61; MSSA 17; mTaira 44; Myibean 82; N.Minton 52; naka-stockphoto 11; Namart Pieamsuwan 47; Natalia D. 66; Nattee Chalermtiragool *cover*; Nattika 86; natu 13; Nawanon 68; Neale Cousland 32; Ned Snowman 31; Nerthuz 33; Nerthuz 64; Nghia Khanh 73; Nicole Kwiatkowski 73; nik7ch 14; Nikki Zalewski 22; Nikolas_jkd 38; NIPAPORN PANYACHAROEN 85; ntstudio 82; nui7711 57; number-one 21, 74, *back cover*; NYS 28; oatawa 39; odd-add 42; Odua Images 39, 40, 76; Oksana Mizina 83; oksana2010 67; Oleksandr Yuhlchek 55; Oleksandra Naumenko 79; Olesia Bilkei 37; Olga Kashubin 73; Oliver Foerstner 32, cover; Ollinka 37; onair 82; optimarc 85; ostill 64; OZaiachin 60; Palis Michalis 54; panda3800 82; pang_oasis 33; Paolo Bona 68; pathdoc 84; Patrick Foto 72; Patrick Krabeepetcharat 76; paulaphoto 12; pcruciatti 56; Pepsco Studio 50; Peter Hermes Furian 73; Phattana Stock 38; phive 86; photka 47; photo5963_shutter 25; Photographee.eu 15; photomaster 67; PhotoRoman 72; photosync 67; Phovoir 74; Phuong D. Nguyen 30; Picnote 33; Picsfive 80, 82; pinunpa 30; pio3 69; Pixel Embargo 27; PORTRAIT IMAGES ASIA BY NONWARIT 20; PR Image Factory 15; Praisaeng 75; Prasit Rodphan 48; Pressmaster 44, 68; Preto Perola 46; PrinceOfLove 58, 80; ProfStocker 43; pryzmat 27; PSboom 72; PT Images 13; racorn 48; rangizzz 82; atmaner 37; Rawpixel.com 32, 65, 70; Rido 76; risteski goce 33; Rob Wilson 30; Roman.Volkow 39; Romaset 82; RossHelen 28; RPBaiao 72; RTimages 38; Rudchenko Liliia 84, 86; rvlsoft 56; Ryszard Stelmachowicz 37; S-F 67; Sagase48 70; saiko3p 82; Sakarin Sawasdinaka *front flap*; Sakuoka 27; Santibhavank P 62; sasaken 37; Sathit 77; Scanrail1 46, 80; ScriptX 79; Sean Heatley 72; Sean Locke Photography 40; Sean Pavone 30, 72; sezer66 65; Shanti Hesse 70; Shin Okamoto 44, endpaper; Shinari 77; shopplaywood 34; showcake 86; Shumo4ka 22; Silvy78 83; Sinseeho 16; Sivapoom Yamasaki 52; skyfish 42; Smileus 42; sociologas 22; Solomatina Julia 22; SOMMAI 84; Son Hoang Tran 61; Sonya illustration 22; Sorbis 79; spaxiax 78; spiber.de 46; Spotmatik Ltd 62; ssuaphotos 62; Stanislav Simonov 56; Stanislav Khokholkov 74; steamroller_blues 81; stockofter 76; stockphoto mania 30; stockphoto-graf 81; Stone36 37; Stuart Jenner 10, 21, 58, 82; Studio KIWI 86; studioloco 43; Sukpaiboonwat *cover*; Susan Schmitz 71; swissmacky 34; Syda Productions 30, 70; Sylvie Bouchard 56; szefei 13, 46, 68, 75; tab62 13; takayuki 10, 12, 21, *cover, endpaper*; tanuha2001 56, 80; Tanya Sid 78; taveesak srisomthavil 42; Teguh Mujiono 17; TENGLAO 75; testing 79; Thanit Weerawan 81; The Len 43; theerasakj 13; themorningglory 70; Tim UR 83; timquo 83; Tobik 84; Tom Wang 10, 16, 36, 44, 46, 49, 64; Tony Magdaraog 75; TonyV3112 79; Tropper2000 82; TTstudio 65; ucchie79 13; Valdis Skudre 36; Valentina Razumova 78; Valentyn Volkov 78, 82; vandycan 29; vasabii 52; vectorshape 55; Veronica Louro 82; vhpfoto 36; vipman 15; viravi 83; Vitaly Korovin 19; Vitchanan Photography 52; Vlad Teodor 28; Vladimir Wrangel 67; Vladislav S 83; Volosina 86; wacpan 45; Wallenrock 80; wavebreakmedia 24, 58, 61, 68; WDG Photo 64; wong yu liang 59; WPixz 77; xmee 72; Yangxiong 33; YanLev 45; Yuri Samsonov 80; Zacarias Pereira da Mata 37; zcw 81; zeljkodan 45; Zerbor 63; zhu difeng 30; ZinaidaSopina 30; ZQFotography 58; Zush 85

Published by Tuttle Publishing, an imprint of Periplus
Editions (HK) Ltd

www.tuttlepublishing.com

Copyright © 2018 Periplus Editions (HK) Ltd

ISBN: 978-4-8053-0899-8

25 24 23   10 9 8 7
Printed in China   2306EP

"Books to Span the East and West"

Tuttle Publishing was founded in 1832 in the small New
England town of Rutland, Vermont [USA]. Our core values
remain as strong today as they were then—to publish
best-in-class books which bring people together one page
at a time. In 1948, we established a publishing outpost in
Japan—and Tuttle is now a leader in publishing English-
language books about the arts, languages and cultures of
Asia. The world has become a much smaller place today
and Asia's economic and cultural influence has grown.
Yet the need for meaningful dialogue and information
about this diverse region has never been greater. Over
the past seven decades, Tuttle has published thousands
of books on subjects ranging from martial arts and
paper crafts to language learning and literature—and our
talented authors, illustrators, designers and photographers
have won many prestigious awards. We welcome you to
explore the wealth of information available on Asia at
www.tuttlepublishing.com.

Distributed by

North America, Latin America &
Europe
Tuttle Publishing
364 Innovation Drive
North Clarendon,
VT 05759-9436 U.S.A.
Tel: 1 (802) 773-8930
Fax: 1 (802) 773-6993
info@tuttlepublishing.com
www.tuttlepublishing.com

Japan
Tuttle Publishing
Yaekari Building, 3rd Floor
5-4-12 Osaki
Shinagawa-ku
Tokyo 141-0032
Tel: (81) 3 5437-0171
Fax: (81) 3 5437-0755
sales@tuttle.co.jp
www.tuttle.co.jp

Asia Pacific
Berkeley Books Pte. Ltd.
3 Kallang Sector #04-01/02
Singapore 349278
Tel: (65) 6741-2178
Fax: (65) 6741-2179
inquiries@periplus.com.sg
www.tuttlepublishing.com

How to Download the Online Audio recordings for this Book.

1. Make sure you have an Internet connection.
2. Type the URL below into your web browser.

http://www.tuttlepublishing.com/japanese-picture-dictionary-downloadable-content

For support, you can email us at info@tuttlepublishing.com.

三味線
shamisen
a banjo-like lute with
three strings

子供の日
Kodomo no hi
Children's Day
(a Japanese holiday)

お好み焼き
okonomiyaki
Japanese savory
pancake

書道
shodō
calligraphy

祝う
iwau
to congratulate;
to celebrate

扇子
sensu
fan

コロッケ
korokke
croquettes

超高層ビル
chōkōsō biru
skyscraper